Clan Battles

Clan Battles

Warfare in the Scottish Highlands

Chris Peers

Pen & Sword
MILITARY

First published in Great Britain in 2023 by
Pen & Sword Military
An imprint of Pen & Sword Books Limited
Yorkshire – Philadelphia

ISBN 978 1 39907 003 4

A CIP catalogue record for this book is
available from the British Library

Typeset by Mac Style
Printed in the UK by CPI Group (UK) Ltd, Croydon, CR0 4YY.

MIX
Paper | Supporting
responsible forestry
FSC® C013604
FSC www.fsc.org

Pen & Sword Books Limited incorporates the imprints of After the
Battle, Atlas, Archaeology, Aviation, Discovery, Family History,
Fiction, History, Maritime, Military, Military Classics, Politics,
Select, Transport, True Crime, Air World, Frontline Publishing,
Leo Cooper, Remember When, Seaforth Publishing, The Praetorian
Press, Wharncliffe Local History, Wharncliffe Transport,
Wharncliffe True Crime and White Owl.

For a complete list of Pen & Sword titles please contact

PEN & SWORD BOOKS LIMITED
47 Church Street, Barnsley, South Yorkshire, S70 2AS, England
E-mail: enquiries@pen-and-sword.co.uk
Website: www.pen-and-sword.co.uk
or
PEN AND SWORD BOOKS
1950 Lawrence Rd, Havertown, PA 19083, USA
E-mail: Uspen-and-sword@casematepublishers.com
Website: www.penandswordbooks.com

Contents

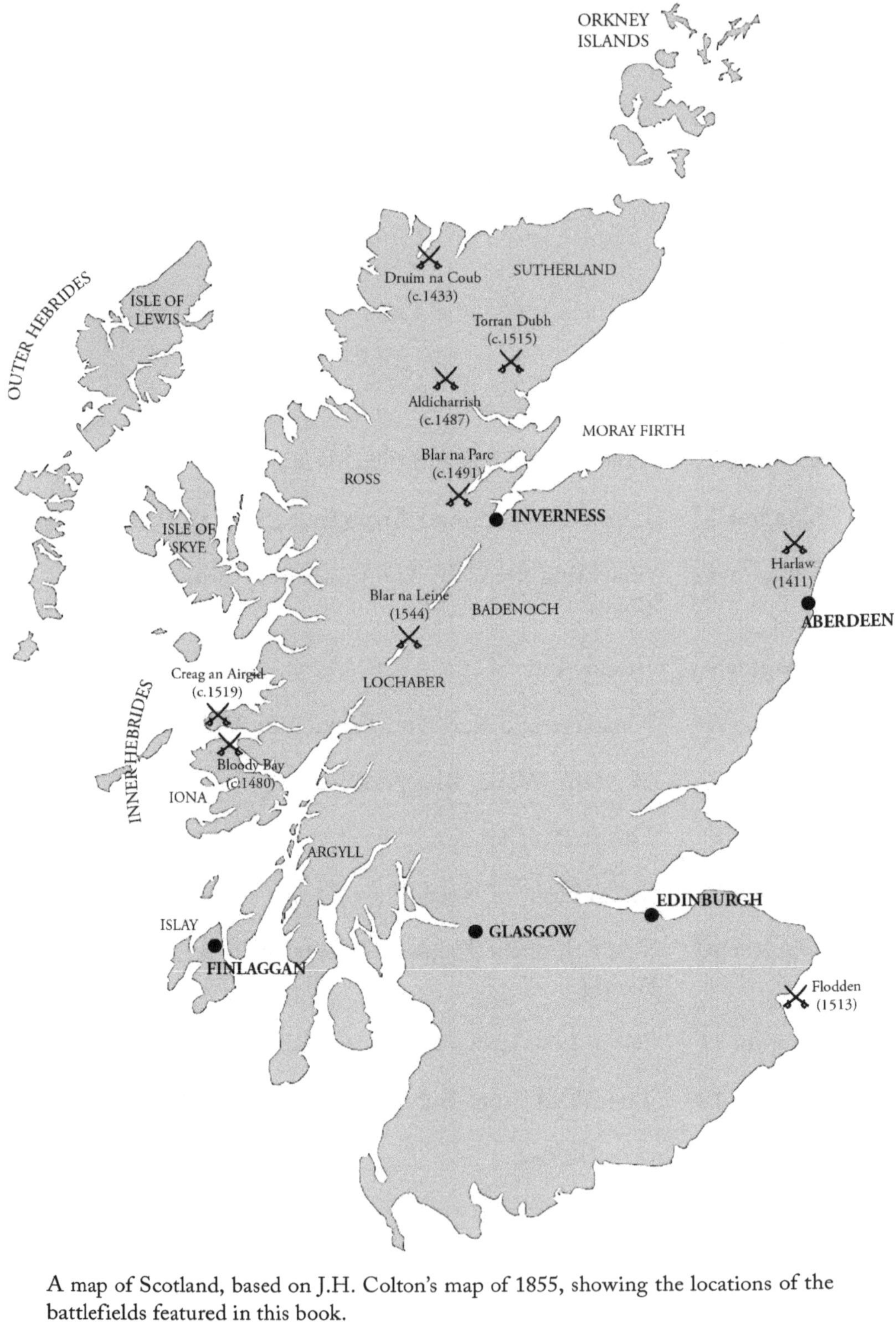

A map of Scotland, based on J.H. Colton's map of 1855, showing the locations of the battlefields featured in this book.

Introduction

This book was conceived as a sequel to my *The Highland Battles*, published by Pen & Sword in 2020, in which I discussed seven of the less well-known encounters that took place in northern and western Scotland in the early part of the Middle Ages, beginning with the Norse conquest of Orkney and Caithness in the ninth century AD, and ending with the Battle of Largs in 1263. I was inspired to write it by the realisation that although Scotland's history is a major attraction for visitors, and many more of its historic battlefields remain in good condition than in more densely populated England, very little is known about most of them. Popular interest in Highland warfare focuses on the seventeenth and eighteenth centuries, and in particular the Jacobite risings of 1715 and 1745, but the region is littered with battle sites from earlier eras, some identified and listed by official bodies like Historic Environment Scotland, a few even marked by memorials on the ground, but most almost completely forgotten. Almost no archaeological work has been done on any of them beyond a few unsuccessful metal-detecting forays. Some sites cannot be identified precisely on the ground, and some, like Aldicharrish (Chapter 6), have been lost to sight under modern forestry plantations, but not even the clearly identifiable ones are very well known or publicised, even locally. I discovered on a recent trip to the Ardnamurchan Peninsula that most visitors, and even many residents, were entirely unaware of the historical significance of Bloody Bay (Chapter 5), a major feature in the landscape that is clearly visible from the southern shore of the peninsula and is the site of the only well-documented naval battle of the clan era. So there is a great deal of territory still to explore, and the seven locations discussed in this volume are only a small selection of the most important, interesting or accessible ones. Two better-known clashes that took place outside the Highlands – Harlaw in 1411 and Flodden in 1513 – have also been discussed at some length because of their importance for the clans that took part in these seven.

Following the precedent of *The Highland Battles*, I have included in each relevant chapter a short paragraph giving details of how to get to the location and what can be seen there today. Where possible, this includes directions for using public transport, but unfortunately, some of these places are very remote and transport links, especially in the far north-west, are infrequent, so travelling by car may be the only realistic option. In this connection, I would like to acknowledge the invaluable assistance of my wife, Kate, who not only drove hundreds of miles on the often narrow and winding Highland roads, but also contributed many helpful observations about the history and topography of the surrounding areas while doing so. If this book achieves anything of what it has set out to do, it is largely thanks to her.

These battles cover a time span of just over a century, from Druim na Coub, which was fought around 1433, to Blar na Leine in 1544. The 170 years between Largs and Druim na Coub were taken up to a great extent with the Scottish Wars of Independence against England, which are far better studied, and mostly took place outside the Highlands. The events of this period in so far as they relate to the Highland clans are discussed briefly in Chapter 1. Geographically, our territory corresponds to what was at the time the Gaelic-speaking Highlands and Islands (sometimes referred to for brevity simply as 'the Highlands'), or approximately the area covered by the modern Scottish Council areas of Highland, Argyll and Bute, and Na h-Eileanan Siar or the Western Isles. Traditionally, this area, including the offshore islands, was divided among the counties of Caithness, Sutherland, Ross, Inverness and Argyll, and these names are still useful as a convenient way of indicating the approximate location of a site. All of these regions were officially under the authority of the Scottish monarchy throughout the period, but in many places the competing ambitions of the MacDonald Lords of the Isles and the sheer remoteness of the northern mountains made this authority little more than nominal. The island groups of Orkney and Shetland featured prominently in the previous book but merit only incidental mentions in this one. This is not because they were not the scenes of frequent warfare, but because they remained largely Scandinavian rather than Celtic, politically until the 1470s and culturally for much longer. They were therefore outside the Gaelic-speaking and clan-based culture area that is the focus here.

The geographical background to Highland warfare has been discussed in more detail in *The Highland Battles*, so here it will suffice to explain that the Atlantic coast, on the western side of the spine of high mountains that runs north to south through the Highlands, is more mountainous and less suitable for agriculture than the shores of the North Sea in the east, and is broken by numerous long inlets or sea lochs. Further west are the islands of the Hebrides, frequently known simply as the Isles, which are often more low lying and fertile; the southernmost of the large ones, Islay, was the principal power base of the lordship of the Isles, and both in the Hebrides and on the adjacent mainland, the military power of the clans was based as much on their fleets of galleys as on their land armies. The Ardnamurchan Peninsula, the most westerly point of the British mainland, divides the west coast and the Isles roughly into northern and southern halves. East of Ardnamurchan, covering both shores of the inlets of the sea known as Loch Linnhe and Locheil and their hinterlands, is Lochaber, a district rich in resources and fighting men, which Martin MacGregor (2012) describes as 'the launchpad for MacDonald expansionism eastwards'. Some of the districts surrounding Lochaber were especially hard of access from outside and provided strategic refuges for the clans that occupied them. Inland from Ardnamurchan and extending northwards, the mainland lying between Loch Sunart in the south and Loch Hourn, opposite Skye nearly 40 miles further north, was traditionally known in Gaelic as Garmoran or Garbh-chriochan, the 'Rough Bounds'. This included the districts of Moidart and Knoydart, and away from the narrow coastal strip was a maze of mountains and bogs that invaders found almost impossible to negotiate. All these areas belonged to the sphere of influence of the MacDonalds, and their ambitions often drew them northwards and eastwards towards Easter Ross and the shores of the Moray Firth, the great inlet of the North Sea on the opposite side of the country. However, their reach never extended to the far north-west of the mainland, now part of the county of Sutherland, where the power base of the formidable Clan Mackay was in Strath Naver, a fertile valley in the midst of windswept moorlands that is protected by its sheer remoteness. Here in the far north, the mountains are more widely scattered and the sea lochs less intrusive than on the west coast, so that the inhabitants were less reliant on the sea for transport. But like the MacDonalds, they often found themselves drawn towards the Moray Firth, taking advantage of the overland routes offered by wide valleys (or straths) like Strath Oykel, Strath Conan and Strath Fleet.

It will be noted that our seven battles cluster in a couple of limited areas. Three of them are in Easter Ross and eastern Sutherland, situated on the more fertile and densely populated side of the country but on the routes leading from the wilder north and west. Two more are almost within sight of each other on the shores of Loch Sunart in Lochaber. Another, Blar na Leine, was fought in the Great Glen, which was the main route between these two districts. The outlier is Druim na Coub on the north coast of Sutherland, whose remote location is explained by the fact that its inhabitants, the Mackays, deliberately allowed invaders from eastern Sutherland to penetrate into the heart of their country before turning on them. Of the six land battles, five were fought in relatively low-lying and settled valleys. Only one, Creag an Airgid on Ardnamurchan, is in the classic wild moorland terrain that we normally associate with the Highlands; this can be explained by the fact that the attackers were intercepted while marching across the peninsula from one coast to the other, but even here the area may have been more populated and better cultivated at the time. These are of course only a sample of the countless battle sites in the Highlands and Islands, some of which are in very different types of terrain, but they do serve to illustrate the principle that here, as elsewhere, campaigns tended to be heavily influenced by geography, and battles were concentrated in particularly desirable areas or on certain well-used strategic routes.

A note on Gaelic names

As is well known, the term 'clan' comes from the Gaelic '*clann*', meaning 'children', and refers to a social or political grouping made up of people who claim descent from a common ancestor. Hence in Scotland, the clans very often share a name beginning in Mac, meaning 'son of-' (the feminine version, Nin or Nean, is less often seen). But in the period under discussion here, these names were not formalised like modern surnames, and as everyone has multiple ancestors, a man could be known as the 'son' of any of them, including his biological father. So, for example, Clan Donald or MacDonald, the descendants of Donald, includes subgroups known as Clanranald (never for some reason Clan MacRanald) and Clan MacIain, whose eponymous founders, Ranald and Iain, were themselves descendants of Donald. But the MacIain brothers Domhull and Iain, whose feats of archery are described in Chapter 3, belonged not to Clan MacIain but to Clan MacRae, from the other members of which they distinguished themselves by using the name of a more recent ancestor. Others were identified by the name of their dwelling place, or by physical descriptors like 'Ban', 'fair'; 'Dubh', 'dark'; or 'Og', 'young'. There is the added complication that by the fifteenth century, the variety of English known as Scots had replaced Gaelic as the language of central government, and so men prominent enough to be named in official documents are generally known to historians by an Anglicised version of their given names. Therefore, Earls Iain and Alasdair of the Isles often appeared, as they do here, as John and Alexander.

I hope that Gaelic-speaking readers will forgive me for preferring clarity over consistency in the use of names, so that characters will be introduced by the names with which they are most commonly associated in the literature, whether this is the Gaelic or the English version. Thus, names beginning with Mac may be rendered as Mc, and the second part may or may not be capitalised, according to the usage of the source or the individual cited. For the same reason I have not tried to be consistent with the spelling of Gaelic words and place names, which have changed dramatically several times since they were first written down. Non-Gaelic speakers will need to be equally tolerant of the omission of any guide to pronunciation, which would take up an excessive amount of space even if I felt competent to provide it. For those who are interested in studying the language, Gaelic is very well provided with good-quality learning materials in the form of books and DVDs. I recommend contacting Comhairle nan Leabhraichean, the Gaelic Books Council, at www.gaelicbooks.org.

Chapter 1

After Largs

In 1266, following the Scottish victory over the Norwegians at the Battle of Largs and the death of King Haakon IV of Norway, the two countries signed the Treaty of Perth, which promised to bring to an end several centuries of war on Scotland's northern and western frontiers. In return for a down payment of 4,000 marks and a small annual rent, Haakon's successor, Eric, ceded to King Alexander III of the Scots the whole of the island chain of the Hebrides, and sealed the bargain by marrying Alexander's daughter, Margaret. (The northern islands of Orkney and Shetland would remain Norwegian until transferred to Scotland by another marriage settlement in 1472.) This was a moment of triumph for Alexander, but it was not to last. His first wife, Margaret, the daughter of King Henry III of England, died in 1275, followed within a few years by all three of their children. In 1285, the king, still only in his forties, married again to Yolande de Dreux, but in the following March he was thrown from his horse and killed while on his way from Edinburgh to Kinghorn in Fife to surprise his new bride on her birthday. The only surviving heir to the throne was now the daughter of the late Queen Margaret of Norway, also named Margaret, who became known as the Maid of Norway. King Edward I of England had already proposed a marriage alliance between young Margaret and his own son, the future Edward II, and so with the prospect of an amicable union between the two kingdoms on the horizon the council of Alexander's magnates arranged for the Maid to be brought to Scotland. Unfortunately, she fell ill and died in Orkney while en route, leaving the country once again without a ruler.

From thirteen distant relatives who proceeded to lay claim to the throne, two front runners soon emerged, both tracing their descent from the daughters of David I, who had died as long ago as 1153. The first to raise an army in support of his ambition was Robert V de Brus or Bruce, the fifth Lord of Annandale, but his rival John Balliol was favoured by many Scots because of his slightly stronger hereditary claim. Fearing a civil war, Bishop William Fraser of St Andrews took the drastic step of writing to King Edward in England and asking him to mediate. The disastrous outcome of this no doubt well-intentioned move is well known; Edward summoned the Scottish nobles to a council at Norham on the border between the two kingdoms and eventually pronounced in favour of Balliol, who became King John I. In return, the latter was obliged to accept Edward as his overlord, but in doing so, he lost the trust of his new subjects, who saw the arrangement as a humiliation for Scotland. The result was decades of war, during which the Scots not only had to contend with repeated English invasions, but also turned on each other with increasing ferocity. One of Balliol's first acts was to confiscate the Bruce lands and give them to one of his own kinsmen, John Comyn. Balliol abdicated in 1296 and Edward attempted to control Scotland directly under a military governor, but a year later, a minor nobleman, William Wallace, led a revolt in the name of King John. Wallace won a spectacular victory at Stirling Bridge in September 1297 and temporarily drove the English out, but was defeated at Falkirk in the following year, and was eventually captured and executed as a traitor. John Comyn briefly became Guardian of Scotland, but in 1306 he was stabbed to death during a parley in a church in Dumfries by Robert V's grandson, the future king, Robert 'the Bruce'.

Six weeks later, Robert was crowned king at Scone in a ceremony attended by the bishops of St Andrews, Moray and Glasgow as well as by many secular magnates. But by no means all Scots supported him, especially as he was under a sentence of excommunication for the sacrilegious murder of Comyn. Bruce defeated an English army at Loudoun Hill in May 1307, and the death of Edward I two months later gained him a valuable respite. He spent much of the next three years fighting against rivals in Scotland, mainly in the Comyn lands in Aberdeenshire, until in 1310 a full council of the Scottish clergy finally recognised him as king. He was then able to concentrate on expelling the surviving English garrisons, of which by the end of 1313 only Stirling remained. The following summer, Edward I's successor, the much less militarily able Edward II, attempted to relieve Stirling, a campaign that led to Robert the Bruce's great victory at Bannockburn in June, and the eventual achievement of freedom from English domination. In the famous Declaration of Arbroath of 1320, addressed to Pope John XXII, the Scottish barons and clergy asserted the independence of their country, and the Pope soon afterwards annulled the sentence of excommunication on their king. Finally, in the Treaty of Northampton of 1328, signed a year before Robert's death, the English themselves recognised Scotland as an independent country.

The Scottish victory had been achieved at a terrible price, however, and part of that price was the intensification of some of the divisions that had already plagued the kingdom in the thirteenth century. During the following century, the fortunes of the various clans of the West Highlands, most of whom claimed to be descended from the sons of the Hebridean warlord Somerled, who had died in 1164, rose or fell depending on the side that they had taken in the wars of Robert I. The MacDougalls had favoured the defeated Comyn faction, and so their lands in Ardnamurchan and Lochaber were confiscated and given to the MacDonald chieftain, John of Islay, whose father Angus had harboured Robert when he was a fugitive after a defeat by the MacDougalls in 1306. John subsequently gained the lordship of Garmoran from his first marriage, which gave him control of the west coast of the mainland as far north as Loch Hourn, and by 1336 he was styling himself 'Lord of the Isles of Scotland' ('*Dominus Insularum*', or, in Gaelic, '*Ri Innse Gall*'). From the beginning, however, this was no ordinary feudal lordship.

From the ninth to the thirteenth centuries, the Hebrides had been part of the Kingdom of the Isles, which although not always united had its main power base on the Isle of Man and maintained close contacts with Ireland. Its rulers were of Norse descent and recognised the overlordship of the kings of Norway, but for much of this period they were de facto independent. Since the Treaty of Perth, the Hebrides had been recognised as belonging to Scotland, while Man had been fought over by the Scots and English, finally coming under the control of the latter in 1346. The title '*Ri Innse Gall*' was thought to have been associated with Somerled, although its origins are much earlier, and it was adopted by several of those who claimed to be his successors over the next hundred years. '*Ri*' (or in modern spelling, *righ*) is a Gaelic term cognate with the word for 'king' in many other Indo-European languages (for example the Latin '*rex*', or French '*roi*') and often – though not exclusively – used in medieval records for sovereign rulers, so the phrase '*Ri Innse Gall*' can be translated equally well as 'lord' or 'king' of the Isles. The use of the title by the MacDonalds was clearly intended to imply continuity with the old Kingdom of the Isles, and thus a degree of independence which was scarcely compatible with the increasingly centralist policies of the government in Edinburgh. This situation was in fact exploited by both sides during the Wars of Independence and afterwards, with the English encouraging the separatist ideas of the Lords of the Isles in the hope of opening a 'second front' against their mutual enemy, the king of Scots (MacGregor, 2012). At the same time, the Scots made use of the historical connection between the Hebrides and Ireland to funnel expendable Highlanders into Ireland to frustrate English ambitions there – a policy first adopted in the years after Bannockburn.

The gallowglass

Gaelic warfare in this period was always overshadowed by events in Ireland, and although many of the clans featured here were not involved in the campaigns there directly, it is difficult to understand the context of Scottish Highland warfare without a brief survey of the Irish wars and the Scottish warriors who fought in them. Warfare in Ireland is a complex subject that merits separate treatment (see Hayes-

McCoy, 1937, Duffy, 2002, and Cannan, 2010), but we will often find that evidence from Irish sources can illuminate aspects of warfare in Scotland. Scots had been serving the Irish kings as bodyguards since the eleventh century (Cannan, 2010), while Irish troops were often involved in the Scottish wars of the twelfth. Since the thirteenth century, if not earlier, men from the Hebrides and the West Highlands had also been travelling to Ireland, sometimes as individuals, but usually in organised companies drawn from specific clans, to take employment as mercenaries, or 'gallowglasses'. The term comes from the Irish '*gall oglaich*', or 'young foreign warrior', and first appears in 1290 to describe MacDonnel mercenaries fighting in Ireland. (See page 36 for the use of the same word for a chief's bodyguard in Scotland.)

Since Henry II of England's invasion in 1171, the Irish had been fighting not only each other but also the English, and the Scots were drawn further into the conflict in 1315, when Edward Bruce, the brother of King Robert, landed in Ireland and proclaimed himself High King. He was defeated and killed by an Anglo-Irish army three years later, at the Battle of Faughart, but the tradition of Highland warriors seeking employment in Ireland was by then firmly established, and over the next three centuries, Scottish gallowglasses exploited the island as a source of loot and a training ground for battle. Several of the war leaders who feature in our story had learned their trade in Ireland, notably Donald Balloch of the MacDonalds, who defeated the government forces at Inverlochy in 1431. The most prominent clans involved in the business were the MacSweens, MacDowells and MacDonnels from Argyll in the south-west, a district that had always had close ties to Ireland. (The name MacDonnel is obviously related to MacDonald, and the MacSweens were also originally a branch of that clan.) The MacCabes and MacRorys from the Hebrides were prominent too, and men from most other clans could be found serving as individuals or in small bands.

The equipment and style of fighting of the gallowglass inevitably resembled those of his counterparts at home in the Highlands. His principal weapon had originally been a spear, but by the fourteenth century, he had become closely associated with the two-handed axe (Heath, 1982). The leaders of the gallowglass bands often presented themselves in poetry as liberators, fighting to free the original Irish homeland of their own Gaelic culture from the English oppressors. In reality, their men oppressed the Irish people almost as blatantly themselves, taking full advantage of the privilege of 'coyne and livery', which meant that they were billeted by their employers on the local peasantry and fed at their expense. The galley fleets that conveyed gallowglasses to and from Ireland also frequently indulged in cattle stealing and other opportunistic crimes. Their swansong came with Elizabeth I's campaigns in Ireland in the late sixteenth century, when they found their old-fashioned tactics of little use against English pikemen and cavalry, and the era of the gallowglass finally ended with the defeat of the Irish lords after the Battle of Kinsale in 1601.

The Wolf of Badenoch

In 1337, the Hundred Years War broke out between England and France, and in 1346, Robert the Bruce's successor, King David II, was persuaded to go to war with England again to support the French. David, however, was poorly supported by his fractious subjects and was captured by the English at the Battle of Neville's Cross, near Durham. He remained in prison for eleven years until his ransom was paid, leading to a power vacuum in Scotland, which allowed John, the Lord of the Isles, to extend his rule even further. In 1350, John divorced his wife and married Margaret, the daughter of David's nephew Robert Stewart, High Steward of Scotland, who was acting as regent during David's imprisonment. When David died childless in 1371, Robert succeeded to the throne as Robert II and confirmed his son-in-law John in possession of all the lands that he controlled, including those inherited from his first wife. John's meteoric career thus gave rise to a very strong regional power in the north and west of Scotland, which was to be a thorn in the side of the monarchy for more than a century, and the situation only became more contentious in the next generation.

In the late fourteenth century, another superficially similar power arose in the eastern Highlands – Alexander Stewart, an illegitimate son of Robert II, who became known in Gaelic as Alasdair Mor Mac an Righ, 'Big Alexander, the son of the king', and in English by the sinister nickname of 'the Wolf of Badenoch'. Although he was not a Highlander himself, his career was to influence forever the perception of the Highlands in the country at large. It seems that he had received the lordship of Badenoch from his father, and by 1370, he was established at Ruthven, where we know that he issued a proclamation promising to protect the lands and tenants of the Bishop of Moray. Over the next few years, Robert gave his son further grants of land, making him his royal lieutenant in the north, with authority, at least in theory, as far afield as Sutherland and Caithness.

It may have seemed to King Robert that the best way to govern the Highlands and Islands was to delegate authority to the two most powerful men in the region – John MacDonald in the west and Alexander Stewart in the east. But the arrangement was not to last, in part because of the utter failure of one of them to govern responsibly. In 1382, the Wolf of Badenoch married Euphemia, the widow of Sir Walter Leslie, the late earl of Ross, and took the lands of the earldom under his control, at the same time acquiring the title of earl of Buchan. He now had a claim to possess land as well as delegated authority over most of northern Scotland, which he ruled from his castle at Lochindorb, in the hills south of the Moray Firth. According to his biographer Alexander Grant (1993), the Wolf now held more power on the Highland mainland than anyone since the reign of MacBeth in the eleventh century. He at once set about abusing this power, raising a private army of '*caterans*', soldiers of fortune from all over the Highlands, with which he terrorised his neighbours. Complaints began to reach King Robert about his son's unauthorised seizure of castles and alleged involvement in murders and robberies, as well as his diversion of revenues intended for the Crown into his own pockets, but the king ignored them.

Alexander's relations with the Bishop of Moray, Alexander Bur, had been deteriorating since 1380, when the two men had disputed the control of some church lands in Badenoch. Bur had tried to have the case held in court in Inverness, but as the Sheriff of Inverness was none other than the Wolf of Badenoch himself, it is not surprising that the judgement went against him. The bishop successfully appealed to the king and the disputants were officially reconciled, but the Wolf was clearly angry that anyone had dared to stand up to him. Furthermore, Bur had taken the side of Euphemia, who had complained to the bishop about her husband's cruelty and infidelity, and in 1389, the Wolf was made to promise that he would leave the mistress with whom he had been living, return Euphemia's possessions and abstain from threatening to kill her. In the following year, apparently in retaliation for this humiliation, the Wolf and his *caterans* attacked the towns of Forres and Elgin. The sack of Elgin was a crime that soon became notorious, especially because it was seen as a deliberate act of revenge against the bishop and the Church. In the presence of Alexander, and apparently on his orders, his *caterans* burned the town, including a hospice, eighteen mansions belonging to the clergy, and the famous cathedral, with all the valuable books and documents kept there. But King Robert had died just before the attack, and without his protection, Alexander was gradually stripped of much of his power. In 1392, the Pope granted Euphemia a separation, which deprived her husband of the revenues of the earldom of Ross, and by 1394, Sir Walter's son, Alexander Leslie, had reclaimed his birthright as earl.

The Wolf died in 1405, and what is believed to be his tomb can still be seen in Dunkeld Cathedral. The damage to the reputation of the Highlanders who followed him, however, had already been done. Andrew of Wyntoun, writing soon afterwards, condemned in verse the 'wyld wykkyd Heland-men' who had sacked Elgin, and the word '*cateran*', which in Gaelic simply denoted a lightly armed soldier (see Chapter 2), soon became a synonym for barbarism. (For a good account of the Wolf's career, see Grant, 1993).

Red Harlaw

Meanwhile in the west, the MacDonalds were already moving into the power vacuum that the Wolf's demise had left. John of the Isles' son Donald, who had succeeded him as second Lord of the Isles, had married Mary, the sister of Alexander Leslie, and when Alexander died in 1402, Donald put forward his own claim to the earldom of Ross on Mary's behalf. Ross at that time comprised a huge area stretching from the coast of what is now Wester Ross eastwards to the Moray Firth, and if Donald had been able to add it to the lordship of the Isles, he would have been powerful enough to present a serious threat to the Scottish Crown. The run of bad luck that had afflicted the monarchy since David II's reign continued; Robert II was succeeded by his son, Robert III, who was already middle-aged and in poor health, and by the close of the century, power was largely in the hands of another regent, the king's younger brother, Robert, duke of Albany. King Robert died in 1406 but his 12-year-old son, James I, was captured by the English on his way to France and held captive for the next eighteen years, while Albany remained in control at home. The regent was an able and ruthless man who has often been suspected of deliberately delaying the collection of the ransom demanded for the king in order to prolong his own hold on power. He was certainly not prepared to tolerate the formation of a rival power bloc on the scale that Donald of the Isles was planning, and so in order to frustrate this he took control of Ross himself, ruling on behalf of Alexander's heiress, the young Countess Euphemia, who was Albany's granddaughter as well as being Donald's niece. Euphemia had taken her vows as a nun and so was barred from holding the title herself. It should legally have reverted to her aunt, Mary, who was married to Donald, but Albany pressured her into agreeing to transfer it to his own son, the earl of Buchan. The consequent rivalry between the kings of Scotland and the Lords of the Isles over Ross was to be the cause of frequent conflict over the next 130 years, leading to no fewer than eight full-scale wars.

The most dramatic and celebrated of these clashes was the Battle of Harlaw, fought in 1411 between the men of the Isles under Donald and an army led by Earl Alexander of Mar, who was Albany's nephew and an illegitimate son of the Wolf of Badenoch. Donald gathered his forces at Ardtornish Castle, on the Morvern Peninsula on the west coast, and marched north-east up the Great Glen. He defeated an army led by Angus Dubh Mackay at Dingwall and captured the castle there. He then sacked Inverness before swinging south-east and advancing on Aberdeen. As the town was not part of the disputed territories of Ross, it is not clear what his objective was, but it has often been suggested that he was aiming at no less than the overthrow of Albany and the seizure of the throne (Sadler, 2005). In the event, he was intercepted by Mar at Harlaw, near Inverurie, about 12 miles from Aberdeen. The resulting battle was exceptionally hard-fought and bloody, hence the names of 'Red' or 'Bloody' Harlaw by which it was commonly known, though it probably did not involve 50,000 Highlanders or last for six whole days, as was claimed by one of the popular ballads that circulated in the sixteenth century. Sadler estimates that MacDonald may have fielded between 5,000 and 6,000 men, and Mar 3,000 to 4,000, but even these numbers would have dwarfed any of the other clan battles of the age.

Harlaw was long remembered in folklore as the archetypal clash between the 'civilised' Lowlanders and the 'barbarians' of the north and west. John Major, writing a century later, recalled that when he was at school in Aberdeen, 'we were wont to form ourselves into opposite sides, and say that we wanted to play at the battle of Harlaw' (Major, 1892). The course of the fighting is not known in detail, though the later ballads tell us that an initial charge by the Highlanders drove back Mar's men, but the latter managed to rally and a furious melee ensued which lasted until dusk, with neither side gaining any clear advantage (Sadler, 2005). Major went on to say that the common people believed that the 'Wild Scots', as he invariably described the Highlanders, were defeated, but in fact the fight seems to have been a draw, with both sides exhausted at the end of the day. It was Donald, however, who withdrew the next morning and abandoned his campaign. Mar then marched into Ross, recaptured Dingwall Castle and forced Donald to recognise Buchan's claim to the earldom. (Unlike most of the battles discussed in this book, the site of Harlaw is marked by a monument, situated about 2 miles north-west of Inverurie, Aberdeenshire. It can be reached by a minor road off the B9001 at grid reference NJ751241.)

Donald died around 1423 and was succeeded by his son Alexander, styled the third Lord of the Isles. In the following year, King James I returned from captivity in England and immediately took action to curb the excessive power of the Albany family, executing Robert's successor, Duke Murdach, and several of his family for treason. Even though Alexander of the Isles was one of the jury that found them guilty, this did not guarantee him royal favour. Still in pursuit of the elusive earldom of Ross, the third lord is said to have begun negotiations with the king of Norway, hoping to transfer his allegiance. This illustrates the confusion prevalent at the time regarding the status of the lordship, which its possessors seem to have regarded as entitled to conduct its own foreign policy entirely independently of the Scottish monarchy. However, James was in no doubt about where Alexander's loyalty ought to lie. In 1428, he marched north to Inverness with an army, and summoned every Highland chief of note – some fifty in all – to attend a parliament. Those whom he regarded as the leading troublemakers were then brought into the king's presence one by one and placed under arrest. Several of them were summarily executed while others, including Neil Mackay, son of the Angus Dubh who had opposed Donald before Harlaw, were imprisoned on the Bass Rock in the Firth of Forth – Scotland's Alcatraz, from where the cold seas and treacherous currents made escape virtually impossible. Alexander, however, was taken to Perth and detained at the royal court, from where he either escaped or was released within a few months. He then returned to the Isles and raised an army with which he sacked Inverness, but James went after him in person and led his army into Lochaber. There Alexander's forces disintegrated in 1429 when his allies, the clans Cameron and Mackintosh, saw the royal standard unfurled and refused to take the field against the king. The third lord had no choice but to offer his submission and meekly go back into imprisonment, this time in the formidable Tantallon Castle, within sight of the Bass Rock on the East Lothian coast.

But in 1431, Donald Balloch, chief of the branch of the clan known as the MacDonalds of Dunyvaig and the Glens, and one of Alexander's leading vassals, again raised the standard of rebellion. He sailed his fleet up Loch Sunart and surprised the earl of Mar, the royal lieutenant in command of the north, at Inverlochy, near present-day Fort William in Lochaber. He scattered Mar's army with the aid of 200 expert archers recruited from the MacDonalds of Keppoch, but when King James came north once more, most of the chiefs submitted yet again rather than support Donald, who was forced to flee to Ireland. The king put a price on his head, but the MacDonalds refused to betray him. They later claimed that they had beheaded six Campbells before finding one whose features and hair colour were a close enough match to convince James that the rebel was dead. The Campbells were already one of the leading clans of Argyll and were destined to rise much further by exploiting royal patronage. They had been held responsible for the murder of Donald Balloch's father and so the attack on them was no doubt considered to be a form of justice. In fact, Donald long outlived the king, returned home after James's death, and died peacefully in Islay in about 1476.

Highlands and Lowlands

Not all of Scotland's troubles were political. From 1315 onwards, the climate in Europe took a turn for the worse, and a series of bad seasons and livestock epidemics caused famine across most of the continent. This was the beginning of what was to become known as the 'Little Ice Age', which was to last until the nineteenth century. As average temperatures dropped and rainfall increased, agriculture on the northern margins of Europe became less reliable and people reverted to an older tradition of semi-nomadic stock raising, moving with their cattle to upland pastures in the spring to take advantage of the abundant grass and returning to more permanent settlements in the autumn. It is known that settlements elsewhere in Europe retreated from higher altitudes, and although evidence from Scotland is lacking, it is likely that this also happened here (Lamb, 1977). It has been plausibly suggested that this helped to accentuate the growing differences between the Scottish Highlanders and their Lowland neighbours, and by obliging the former to compete for increasingly scarce resources, it may have contributed to their warlike reputation (Miller, 2012).

The shocking mortality of the Black Death, which arrived in 1349, and according to the contemporary *Gesta Annalia* killed around a third of the population, may have further encouraged a move towards dispersed settlements and away from arable farming, which required large numbers of workers to live in dangerous proximity to each other. Against this background, it is perhaps not surprising that the clans of the north and west seem to have consciously emphasised archaic motifs, harking back to semi-mythical Irish or Norse heroes and glorifying the cattle-stealing ethos of epics like the *Tain Bo Cuailnge*, or *Cattle Raid of Cooley*, which was probably first written down around the eighth century, but was set in Ireland in the first century AD. Pastoral societies that relied on cattle were often prone to rustling their neighbours' animals, in part because the creatures are expensive to rear but easy to steal. They were usually pastured outdoors and could wander some distance from their owners' homesteads, but they are herd animals that instinctively stay together when stressed, and so are easily rounded up and driven. Unlike sheep or pigs, they can also cover long distances in the course of a night. The necessity of making long journeys on foot into difficult terrain while tending the cattle, and of being armed and prepared to fight in their defence, was an important factor in the military preparedness of the Highlanders. The 'lifting' of the beasts was therefore a common feature of military campaigns in the Highlands, whether or not that was their prime objective. Christopher Duffy (2015) quotes the earl of Albemarle, writing in

1747, who argued that cattle rustling was 'a sure and known means of training up a number of men in the use of arms, who on the least prospect of plunder are ready to join in any rebellion or tumult'. The operation was not always without danger, however. Donald Sage (1889) tells of one raid in which the Mackays raided the Strath of Kildonan in Sutherland and ran off a herd of cattle belonging to their enemies, the Gunns, but while they were being penned, a bull gored to death the man who was guarding them and the whole herd escaped back to Kildonan. The cattle of the Isles, which bred them in great numbers thanks to their abundant grass and lack of wolves, were small beasts, with long shaggy coats and long horns like present-day Highland cattle (Bingham, 1991), but are invariably described in contemporary accounts as black in colour.

But despite the reputation they had earned through association with people like the Wolf of Badenoch, the Highlanders were never as different from their Lowland neighbours as the latter liked to claim. It has been pointed out (Broun & MacGregor, 2007) that late medieval accounts such as those of the fourteenth-century chronicler John of Fordun are clearly influenced by the classical stereotype of 'civilised' versus 'barbarian' races, which was familiar from Greek and Roman writers. The well-known Gaelic phrase '*Mi run mor nan Gall*', or 'the great ill-will of the Lowlander' (i.e. for the Gaelic-speaking Highlander) probably dates to the eighteenth century, but the sentiment is certainly older. William Dunbar, whose 'flyting' or poetic war of words with Walter Kennedy was performed before James IV around 1500, describes his opponent as speaking like a Highlander, and considers this to justify the scurrilous accusation that he has committed bestiality with horses (Kinsley, 1979). Martin Martin of Skye, writing in the 1690s, complains that 'foreigners, sailing through the Western Isles' were often influenced by the rugged landscape into thinking that 'the inhabitants, as well as the places of their residence, are barbarous' (Martin, 1999), a prejudice that was only strengthened by the fact that the people spoke a different language from the rest of Britain. The language divide within Scotland was relatively recent; in the eleventh century, MacBeth and his court, for example, spoke the same Gaelic tongue as the people of the west coast and the Isles, which in its medieval form was descended from the Old Irish spoken by the earliest kings of a united Scotland in the ninth century, modified and slightly simplified under later Norse influence.

But around 1070, King Malcolm III married an English princess, the future Saint Margaret, and under her influence the court became increasingly Anglicised. The upper classes quickly followed the royal trend, especially in the following century when large numbers of English, Norman and Flemish landowners and entrepreneurs flooded into the more hospitable parts of the country. So gradually, the common people of the Lowlands also began to supplement and then replace their Gaelic with the variant of northern English that came to be known as Scots (see 'The Lost Gaidhealtacht', in Barrow, 1992). By the late fifteenth century, the dividing line between Scots and Gaelic seems to have followed roughly the geographical 'Highland line', which separates the two parts of Scotland, and those living on either side of it were beginning to think of each other as alien. The Lowlanders, or 'householding Scots' as John Major calls them, considered themselves superior 'in dress, in the manner of their outward life, and in good morals' to the so-called 'Wild Scots', a more warlike people 'born in the forests and mountains of the north', who spoke what Major calls 'the Irish tongue'. Bishop Leslie of Ross, writing later in the sixteenth century, does not even accept the Highlanders as being Scots, but refers to them as 'the Irishmen dwelling in the Highlands and Isles of Scotland' and complains of their 'wild, unquiet and unstable nature' (Leslie, 1830). On the other hand, the Gaelic speakers were increasingly cut off from the court and centres of government by the language barrier. (The last Scottish king to speak the language of his northern countrymen was probably James IV, who died in 1513.) They were aware that the country further south had once been Gaelic speaking, and often misinterpreted this as the result of past aggression by the Lowlanders, who had pushed their ancestors off the best land and driven them into the hills (Stevenson, 1980). This of course provided a further incentive, if any were needed, for the cattle-stealing raids into the Lowlands, which remained a source of grievance until the eighteenth century.

Although some districts did enjoy a reputation for being 'far from the law', even in periods of weak central government the Highlands were never a complete free-for-all. Since the Treaty of Perth, the whole of Scotland, apart from Orkney and Shetland, had been theoretically subject to the kings of Scots in Edinburgh, and consequently most of the clan chiefs held their lands through some sort of legal framework. As we have seen, until the end of the fifteenth century, the Lords of the Isles frequently acted as de facto independent rulers, issuing their own charters and even holding negotiations with foreign states despite the uncertainty surrounding their precise relationship to the Scottish Crown. However, at the same time, they maintained a precarious stability in regions that the monarchy, because of its lack of ships and harbours to service them on the west coast, was unable to rule directly. Furthermore, it was an unfortunate habit of both the kings of Scots and the Lords of the Isles to reward those loyal to them at minimal cost to themselves by making grants of lands which they themselves did not control, and which the recipient could only occupy by force against the wishes of the current inhabitants. At the same time, local magnates like the Wolf of Badenoch and the earls of Ross, Huntly and Argyll might hold official positions as agents of royal authority and wield similar powers, while there was no mechanism of royal oversight to prevent them from acting largely in their own interests. An additional source of instability was the traditional practice of handfasting, which involved a man and woman agreeing to live together for a year in a sort of trial marriage, after which they could choose to either marry or separate. According to Martin Martin, any children born during that year were retrospectively legitimised if the couple then married. Marriage for a fixed term, as opposed to for life, was not prohibited by law until 1609, and seems to have persisted clandestinely in the Highlands for at least another century. But although the Church's rules regarding the form of the marriage ceremony had yet to be strictly codified, the Church authorities did not recognise handfasting relationships, as a priest was generally not present when the agreement was made. Therefore, the offspring of such a relationship, strictly speaking, remained illegitimate and thus not entitled to inherit their father's land or titles. There was, therefore, in many cases room for honest disagreement about who the rightful heir to a deceased chief actually was.

MacDonald (1889) quotes the Scottish lawyer Alexander Tytler (1747–1813) in defence of the conduct of Highlanders faced with these problems. The policy of the Crown, Tytler believed, was generally to keep the clans weak by encouraging them to fight against each other, and when the general lawlessness became intolerable, to grant to some local nobleman – often from the loyal families of Atholl, Huntly or Argyll – a commission of lieutenancy with the mission of putting down the offenders. But the powers of such commissions were very ill defined, and the opportunities for their holders to enrich themselves by confiscating land and goods meant that they were often more eager to foment rebellion than to suppress it. 'It was a consequence of this miserable system', says Tytler, 'that [the Highland chiefs] continued in rebellion, not so much from any unwillingness to acknowledge the authority of government, as from a dread of the influence and misrepresentations of their enemies.'

The frustration and helplessness that the government in Edinburgh must often have felt in the face of constant lawlessness in the Highlands, despite the fact that they had largely contributed to it themselves, is illustrated by the series of decrees that were issued proscribing specific clans. In many cases, these were extremely harsh, amounting in modern terms to genocide. The best-known example is the Commission of Fire and Sword issued against the MacGregors in 1610, prohibiting the use of the clan name and authorising neighbouring chiefs to 'ruit out and extirpate all that race', even including those MacGregors who were their own tenants (Bingham). The practice, however, had begun much earlier. In 1528, James V had issued a commission to the earl of Moray and John, chief of Clan Mackenzie, instructing them to attack Clan Chattan 'and invaid thame to thair uter destructioun, be slauchtir, byrning, drowning, and uthir ways…' (Gordon Donaldson, Scottish Historical Documents, 1970, quoted in Bingham, 1991). Only priests, women and children were to be left alive, because to kill them would be 'inhumanite', but they were to be deported to Shetland or Norway and marooned ashore there, which in the absence of any provision for feeding or sheltering them would probably have been a death sentence in any case. Fortunately, none of these draconian measures seems to have been carried out in their entirety. Clan Chattan continued to thrive and even the MacGregors were eventually reprieved, but no doubt many crimes were committed with impunity by people claiming to be following the king's orders.

The legal background to most of the bloody disputes discussed here was therefore extremely complex, and it is not being unduly patronising to suggest that most of the warriors involved would not have understood it. Their motivations were older and simpler ones; they fought for their clan chiefs or feudal overlords, whether voluntarily or not; they fought for status and glory; they fought for loot; and they fought for revenge for past wrongs, real or imagined, for in this society, the old tradition of the blood feud was still strong. In fact, as Martin Martin records of the Western Isles, it was an integral part of inter-clan relations. It was customary, says Martin, for any chief on his accession 'to give a public specimen of his valour' by leading an expedition against a rival clan with which there was some outstanding dispute, and which would later redress the balance when it was the turn of their own chief to prove himself.

Chapter 2

The Clan Chiefs and their Armies

Landscape and environment

Unlike the situation in earlier periods, from the fifteenth century onwards it becomes possible to reconstruct, if only roughly, the way in which the Highlanders lived and the environment that they inhabited. Overall, they probably had a higher standard of living in the Middle Ages than in later centuries, when overpopulation forced them to rely more heavily on cereal crops, which often failed in the unpredictable climate, and in our period, famine appears to have been rare. Martin Martin says of Bernera and North Uist in the Outer Hebrides that because of the high rainfall, the yield of barley on land well manured with seaweed was so great that people from other parts of the country could not believe it, and that elsewhere in the islands were places where grain was grown in such abundance that it was given away to visitors free of charge. Although beef was a favourite food, the common people more often relied on milk, butter and cheese, and Martin describes a dish of thickened milk that was used on Skye in times of crop failure and, he says, was nutritious enough to keep the people in good health for months. As we have seen, the economy on the mainland in the post-Black Death period was based mainly on raising livestock, although crops such as oats and barley were also grown for local consumption. Deer hunting may have been a pastime for the nobility, but at least in some areas venison was probably more widely available to the ordinary clansmen, as in the case of the Mackays of northern Sutherland. Wildfowl and shellfish were common in places, and on some of the smaller islands, sea birds and their eggs were the principal source of protein, as Martin records of Saint Kilda. Fishing rights over lochs and rivers occur frequently enough in legal records to suggest that freshwater fish were a valued resource, though sea fish were harder to exploit and less predictable. Herring often appeared offshore in vast numbers, so far more were caught than could be eaten locally or got to market elsewhere. Martin, for example, records how on Skye, as late as the 1690s, all the available boats were loaded with herring and barrels of them were on sale on the shore for four pence each, but there were no buyers. Just as often, however, the shoals might desert their usual feeding grounds for no discernible reason, which gave rise to numerous superstitions. For example, Martin says that fishermen all over Scotland believed that if they drew blood during a quarrel on a particular stretch of coast, the fish would immediately desert it for the rest of the season.

The population was overwhelmingly rural; Inverness, on the very edge of the Highlands at the north end of the Great Glen, was the only town of significance, as opposed to the fortified strongholds of the chiefs, and even it had only a few hundred houses (Hunter, 1999). In our period, long-distance trade was scarce, and mostly in the hands of merchants from outside the Highlands. Hunter discusses sixteenth-century records of trade through Inverness, which reveal that exports consisted largely of wool, cattle hides, furs and fish, presumably produced by the clansmen in the neighbouring Highlands, but the names of the burgesses living in the town itself suggest that they were Englishmen or Scottish Lowlanders. The clansmen themselves lived in the glens between the mountains in countless small townships, or rather disorderly clusters of houses, which are nowadays known as clachans. By the sixteenth century, these would be surrounded by open fields divided into arable strips, each of which formed a long, low ridge, or rig, cultivated by a particular tenant and either ploughed with the help of oxen or tilled by hand. These ridges were the origin of the name run-rig, which was applied to this system of land tenure, and traces of them remain in many parts of the Highlands, notably on Skye. In James Hunter's words, they would have been such a prominent feature of the landscape that large areas 'must have had something of the appearance of an ocean petrified at a point when it was affected by a steeply rolling swell'. However, the origins of this system are not clear, and in some places, an earlier type of settlement, with more dispersed homesteads surrounded by enclosed fields, probably persisted until the end of the Middle Ages (Dodgson, 1998). In either case, the cattle and other livestock were pastured on the higher ground beyond the cultivated strips; in spring, they were driven into the hills to take advantage of the fresh grass, while in the autumn they would be returned to lower ground and kept indoors at night. They would probably have been guarded at all times, both to prevent them from straying into the crops and to protect them from wolves or human predators.

The houses in which the people lived are difficult to reconstruct because of a lack of surviving dateable remains, but most were probably similar to the eighteenth- and nineteenth-century 'blackhouses', long single-storey rectangular buildings in which the cattle lived at one end and the people at the other. Several restored nineteenth-century blackhouses can be seen today at Gearrannan and Arnol on the island of Lewis, though these would not necessarily be typical of building styles elsewhere. On the mainland where timber was available, in places like Lochaber and Easter Ross for example, 'cruck houses' built on a wooden frame, or cruck, were common, while in poorer or less windswept regions, the walls could have been made of turf rather than stone. Thatched roofs, however, were probably universal, which helps to explain why raiders found the settlements easy to burn. Hunter suggests that houses may have been better built in earlier centuries than in the nineteenth, when the Clearances were under way and land tenure was less certain, so that people found it inadvisable to expend much effort on building a solid home from which they might soon be evicted. On the other hand, where there was chronic warfare, the situation may have been similar to that on the English border, where constant raiding reduced people to such a state of poverty and insecurity that they were prepared to invest only in houses that could be erected in three or four hours (Durham, 2011).

The 'Great Wood of Caledon'

Until very recently it was widely believed that during the Middle Ages most of the Highlands were still covered with dense primeval forest, only about a hundredth part of which has survived to the present day (see, for example, Darling & Boyd, 1964). Its destruction has been variously blamed on burning by Vikings, or by locals to smoke out wolves or bandits, or on clearance for fuel by eighteenth-century industrialists or for sheep grazing by nineteenth-century landowners. Clearly if the campaigns discussed here had taken place in such a forested landscape it would have had a significant influence on both strategy and tactics, but recent research has begun to give a very different picture. (See Rackham, 2015. There is another excellent summary of the evidence, especially as it relates to Scots Pine, in C. Smout, 'The History and the Myth of Scots Pine' (2014) at www.scottishforestrytrust.org.uk.) The idea of the 'Great Wood of Caledon' originated with the Graeco-Roman geographer Ptolemy, but as Rackham points out, he never visited Scotland. John Major identifies Ptolemy's wood with the forested foothills of what he calls the Alps of Scotland, near to Aberdeen, which must presumably be the Cairngorms. The early sixteenth-century Scottish writer Hector Boece also writes of a great wood inhabited by wild bulls, but the region that he describes was limited to a strip along the southern edge of the Highlands, principally in Menteith and Strathearn. Both these districts are, even today, more wooded than the districts further north and west. Elsewhere, and especially in the remoter parts beyond the Great Glen, moorland was probably predominant even in the Middle Ages. Sixteenth-century legislation was frequently concerned with the depletion of woods, suggesting that this was a visible phenomenon at the time, but the concern of course was with usable timber, especially for shipbuilding, rather than with ground cover as such. Murray (2019) points out that although the remains of ancient trees – especially pine – are common in bogs throughout the Highlands, radiocarbon dating shows that most are more than 4,000 years old, and that the damage had been done at least as much by climate change and the resulting spread of peat bogs as by human activity. One possible source of misunderstanding is the cracked and blackened appearance of wood, which has been immersed in acidic peat for a long time, and this can easily be mistaken for charring by fire. Murray adds that old Gaelic place names often focus on the colours and forms of the landscape when seen from a distance, suggesting that the long lines of sight and spectacular views that we are familiar with today were seldom concealed by continuous forest.

Rackham reaches a similar conclusion, arguing in addition that the Highlands as a whole may not have been much more forested in the late Middle Ages than they are now, but that the modern woods are not necessarily in the same places as their predecessors. He explains that they were not generally enclosed by banks or ditches as they were in the lowland parts of Britain, and usually bordered not on agricultural land, which was always scarce in the Highlands, but on moorland or pasture. Furthermore, the trees of which they were composed were mostly Scots pines, which reproduce from windblown seeds, and birches, which are pioneer species with a short lifespan and a preference for open ground. The result was that Highland woods were not fixed to one spot, but wandered across the landscape over generations as new trees sprouted beyond the shade cast by their declining predecessors. Their boundaries were also consequently ill-defined and edged by scrub of varying height and density, so that 'often one cannot say that one acre is woodland and another not' (Rackham). On the other hand, it is difficult to ignore completely the accounts related by Ritchie (1920) and Darling and Boyd of named forests being burned in historic times to destroy the hideouts of wolves, rebels or bandits. These range geographically from Atholl, on the south-eastern edge of the Perthshire Highlands, to Lochaber in the west, and in time from the 1650s, when General Monk is said to have ordered woods cut down near Aberfoyle, to the Second World War, when Darling says that 'the old pines of Lochiel Old Forest [in Lochaber] went up in smoke during Commando training'. It is worth noting that unlike native deciduous trees, Scots pines will burn while standing (Rackham). They have evolved to regenerate after fire so this will not necessarily destroy the woods permanently, but if the land is then overgrazed by deer or sheep, this will prevent the growth of new trees. All this makes it impossible to judge from the appearance of battle sites today whether or not they had any tree cover at the time of the battle, though sometimes old accounts suggest the presence of woods of some sort in places where they are now absent (for example, see Chapter 4 for the Battle of Druim na Coub). It also suggests that when we read of ambushes being laid in woods, as at Druim na Coub, we should probably imagine warriors not hiding behind large trees, but lying prone among saplings and clumps of tall heather, which would have hardly impeded their movements or blocked the flight of their arrows, allowing for a sudden and unexpected attack to be launched from very close range. It is not surprising that such ambushes were a favourite tactic in Highland warfare (Younger, 2012).

Drainage is another factor that could be of great importance on a battlefield, but is difficult to evaluate. Battles and campaigns in many parts of the world have been heavily influenced by the availability of drinking water, and water supplies are often military objectives in themselves, but the Scottish Highlands and Islands are a region of high rainfall and low evaporation, where scarcity of water was seldom an issue. More often, water in its various forms was an obstacle or even a trap. Accounts of retreating forces being caught and slaughtered while crossing rivers and streams are common in theatres of war across the world, and in wet climates, more transient features could be equally deadly. At all times of the year, the visitor to any of the Highland battlefields is likely to encounter boggy conditions, and it is easy to imagine the difficulties they would present for men trying to move quickly and keep their footing during combat while wearing heavy armour and, in many cases, smooth-soled leather footwear. Paul Younger points out that whereas victory in warfare 'depends crucially on knowing the lie of the land and the likely ground conditions of the battlefield', the presence or otherwise of groundwater or bog will vary according to the time of year and weather conditions, and is much harder to spot from a distance than the more obvious battlefield features such as hills or woods. Constantly wet ground in the Highlands can often be identified from a distance in summer and autumn by the conspicuous white flowers of bog cotton (*Eriophorum angustifolium*), but this is not always reliable. What Younger calls 'seepage zones' – where the slope of a hill intersects the underlying water table – can spread over a large area but tend not to have a constant depth of water that is sufficient for the growth of specialised marsh plants, so the vegetation consists mostly of 'ordinary terrestrial grasses', which do not reveal the nature of the ground beneath. Furthermore, because groundwater tends to collect on low ground, it is a particular risk to any army employing the classic tactic of seizing the high ground and charging down to attack an enemy below. Of the battles covered in this book, Flodden (Chapter 8) is a well-known example of how this factor could disrupt the best-laid plans, but it also played a decisive role at Blar na Parc (Chapter 7), and possibly a significant one at both Creag an Airgid (Chapter 10) and Blar na Leine (Chapter 11).

This rather untamed landscape was home to a great number of wild creatures, of which the most prominent, as it still is today, was the red deer. John Major speaks of 'an incredible number of stags and hinds' in the forests of his Scottish Alps. The deer contributed to the military activities of the Highlanders in several ways. They provided food on campaign, and hunting them was useful practice in the use of weapons, especially the bow. It was later said of the Mackays that they not only hunted with enthusiasm, but also 'despise those that do not; so that they have venison always in plenty'. Perhaps because of this diet and the physical exercise required to get it, they were 'strong, frugal, capable of enduring great fatigue' (T. Warren, quoted in Duffy, 2015). Before the introduction of accurate firearms, deer were often hunted not by stalking, as they are today, but in large-scale operations in which long lines of men drove the herds into traps enclosed by stone walls. There they were dispatched by the chiefs and their guests, with spears or arrows, often with the aid of specially bred deerhounds. The sixteenth-century writer Robert Lindesay of Pitscottie (1814) tells how in 1529, at a hunt attended by King James V, 'threttie scoir' (i.e. thirty score, or 600) deer, 'with other small beastis', were killed over three days. Wolves, which were common until the seventeenth century and presented a constant threat to livestock if not to the people themselves, were dealt with in a similar way. In 1428, James I issued an edict requiring his nobles to turn out to hunt wolves at least four times a year (Ritchie, 1920). Ritchie also quotes the *History of the Frasers*, which tells how sometime around 1450, Lady Margaret Lyon, the wife of the chief of the Frasers of Lovat, was credited with driving the wolves out of the hills known as the Aird overlooking Inverness. She is said to have been 'a stout bold woman', able to outmarch even the tough clansmen who accompanied her, and stationed herself at a pass ahead of the beaters where she shot at the escaping animals with arrows. A hunt of this kind (known in Gaelic as a *tainchel*) therefore required the mobilisation of much of the fighting power of the clan, and could be a useful cover for a real mobilisation for war – a fact that was exploited, for example, by the earl of Mar in 1715 (Duffy, 2015).

Clan society

The social background of the warriors who made up the clan armies has been examined by Martin MacGregor (2012), who considers that the situation in Scotland was very different from the better-documented one that prevailed in Ireland at the time. Irish armies did have a core of nobles who formed the personal retinue of a chief, and who usually fought as light cavalry, but the other main elements, the '*cethern*' or kerns and the '*gallowglaich*' or gallowglasses (for whom, see Chapter 1), were landless mercenaries supported by 'coyne and livery'. In contrast, in Scotland military service was tied to the clan system, which in turn was based on land, so that men were in effect obliged to fight for their chiefs as a condition of their tenancy agreements. The clan territory was assumed to belong to the chief by right of inheritance, and most of it was allocated to his closest relatives or otherwise favoured individuals. These were the '*daoine uasile*' or gentlemen, sometimes known simply as the '*fine*' or family, the forerunners of what by the seventeenth century was known as the 'tacksman' class (a 'tack' being a written lease). These men would sublet their land to individual farmers and would be responsible for ensuring that they turned out in time of war. In the Isles, their obligations were often expressed in terms of ships and their crews rather than just numbers of men, which may have been a survival from the old Norse system of ship service (Rixson, 1998). There were a few groups like the MacRaes and MacGregors, who served the Mackenzies and Campbells respectively as a sort of hereditary military caste, but they were, nevertheless, landed clans in their own right rather than merely bands of mercenaries. This arrangement has a great deal in common with classic feudalism as practised in Europe in the earlier Middle Ages. John Major blamed it for the poverty of the country, since subtenants who had no security of tenure lacked an incentive to build substantial houses or otherwise improve their holdings.

In practice, however, in the days when a chief's power and status depended on the number of fighting men he could raise, the people were far more valuable than the untenanted land would have been, and so they were unlikely to be evicted without good reason. The ties between chiefs and their tenants were also greatly strengthened by the idea of common ancestry. These ties of kinship were seldom provable by any documentation more reliable than the invented genealogies of the bards, who for example traced the descent of the MacDonalds from the fifth-century Irish hero Conn of the Hundred Battles, and cases were known where men were openly bribed to take the name of a particular chief and so become members of his clan. But if a clansman believed that he was a blood relative of his chief, however distant, this elevated his relationship with him above the ordinary one of servant and master and implied obligations in both directions. Chiefs could, therefore, lose popular support (which in practice probably meant the support of the '*daoine uasile*') for failure to live up to the ideals of generosity and personal conduct that the heroic ethos of clan society expected of them; see, for example, Chapter 11 for the career of Ranald

Gallda of Clan Ranald, who was supplanted as chief partly because of his refusal to feast his supporters in the style to which they were accustomed. MacGregor also addresses the question of how far down the social scale military obligations extended, since there were obviously poor and landless men in clan society whose participation in warfare is seldom documented. Skene (1880) quotes a description of the Isles from the 1590s, which states that only 'gentlemen' were allowed to leave the country on campaigns, while 'labourers of the ground' were to remain at home to ensure that agriculture was not neglected. This suggests that long-distance expeditions, whether carried out by ship or on foot, might include a very high proportion of wealthy and well-equipped men, but this may not have been the case when a clan was defending its home territory, when every man would have been needed and any prohibition on labourers taking the field would presumably not apply.

The Scottish equivalents of the Irish kerns are usually considered to be the '*ceatharn*' or '*caterans*', the lightly armed men who were held to be distinct from their social superiors, the '*daoine uasile*', but it is not clear whether the former can necessarily be identified with the subtenant class and the latter with the tenants in chief above them. According to Christopher Scott Thompson (2018), the military role of the latter was emphasised by their alternative name of '*buannachan*', or warriors. This writer has an interesting discussion on nomenclature, but the term '*buannach*' does not appear in contemporary Scottish accounts, and in Ireland it seems to have been used to describe a mercenary (Nicholls, 2007). We are therefore left with the anomaly that, although the word '*cateran*' has achieved fairly wide currency, there is no generally accepted term in English for the higher status warriors of the Highland armies. Perhaps the best of the possible alternatives is '*duniewassals*', an Anglicisation of '*daoine uasile*' introduced by Sir Walter Scott in his 1825 song 'Bonnie Dundee'. In Ireland, it was one of the tasks of the kerns to finish off enemies who had been knocked to the ground by the axes of the gallowglasses, but Scottish records do not seem to make any tactical distinction, as opposed to a social one, between the '*daoine uasile*' and the '*ceatharn*'. John Major, for example, distinguishes the 'common people' from the richer men who wore metal armour, but does not suggest that there was any formal distinction by rank or tactical role. Obviously it would have made sense to delegate the less well-equipped men to roles requiring speed and mobility, while deploying their heavily armoured contemporaries in the front line in battle, but there is no reason to believe that the term '*cateran*' denoted a particular social group or fighting style. In fact, as discussed above, the word is most often encountered in the writings of Lowland commentators who use it for undisciplined troops, like those employed by the Wolf of Badenoch, who were held to be responsible for such crimes as pillaging and church burning.

Highlanders were often reported to be tall, strongly built men, which could be attributable in part to a high protein diet thanks to their reliance on cattle for meat and milk. John Major says that an Italian observer, the future Pope Pius II, described James I as 'square set, of a full habit', which Major took to imply a degree of corpulence, though he was of average build for a Scot. Denis Rixson (1998) quotes a sixteenth-century description of Donald Dubh's Highlanders in Ireland, of whom 'three thousand of them [were] very tall men', and English descriptions of Scottish gallowglasses serving in Ireland often emphasise their size and strength. To John Dymmok (an English soldier who served in Ireland and wrote *A Treatise of Ireland*, *c.*1600) they were 'men of great and mighty bodies', while Richard Stanihurst (an Anglo-Irish scholar who contributed a history of Ireland to *Holinshed's Chronicles*, *c.*1587) called them 'tall of stature, big of limb, burly of body' (Cannan, 2010). Rixson, however, sensibly doubts that Highlanders were on average much bigger than other men, and quotes Samuel Johnson as remarking that when he visited the Hebrides in the eighteenth century, the tallest men to be seen were those of higher rank. It is also worth noting that contemporary Italian writers made similar comments about the size and strength of the English. The mighty warriors who so impressed fifteenth- and sixteenth-century observers were probably not only picked from among those who could afford to eat large quantities of meat, but wore padded armour and tall helmets designed to make them look bigger than they actually were.

A Highland chief lived in considerable state, and the maintenance of a large household of retainers and officials was essential to his prestige. Martin Martin says that each chief would be accompanied wherever he went by a '*lucht-taeh* or *guard de corps*', which traditionally consisted of twelve 'young gentlemen' chosen from among his close relations. The word '*taeh*' is obviously the Gaelic '*taigh*', meaning a house, and so the '*lucht-taeh*' was directly equivalent to the '*huscarles*' of their Viking predecessors. These gentlemen were trained in various skills, including fighting with sword and shield and shooting with bows and arrows, as well as less strictly military accomplishments like wrestling, swimming and dancing. In the Isles, at least they would also have been expert sailors. A chief would also have an individual bodyguard or armour-bearer known as a 'gallowglass', a term obviously borrowed from Ireland, where the chief's bodyguards were originally recruited from the true '*gall oglaich*' (Nicholls, 2007). This was not really appropriate in Scotland as there the gallowglass was not usually a 'foreign warrior', but more likely to be a member of the clan. The 'lord's gallowglass' was chosen for his size and physical strength, and received a double portion of meat at every meal. In addition, there were a number of civil officers, usually members of specific families associated with particular hereditary professions, who held land in return for their services. The judges appointed by the Lords of the Isles were among these, as often were the clergy. Great chiefs endowed churches and monasteries and sought to control appointments to clerical offices in the same way as any others, which led to the anomalous situation in which a supposedly celibate priesthood could become hereditary. Examples are recorded of parish priests, priors and even a Bishop of the Isles being succeeded by their sons (Bingham, 1991).

Among the other officers maintained by the chiefs were standard-bearers and quartermasters, of whom the latter were traditionally entitled to the hides of all the cattle slaughtered for feasts and ceremonies. A sentinel or 'cockman' was permanently stationed on the roof of the chief's house with the task of challenging any strangers who approached. There were also foresters, domestic stewards, cup-bearers, and purse masters or treasurers. The Lords of the Isles maintained a separate family of harpists, though in less powerful households the bards or poets probably performed both functions. By the late sixteenth century if not before, there were also specialist pipers like the MacCrimmons. The '*sennachie*' was an extremely important figure in any chief's retinue, serving as the guardian of traditional knowledge regarding the history, legends and genealogy of the clan. Martin Martin, who regarded the *sennachies* or 'orators' as the successors of the ancient druids, says that at one time they were greatly respected because their speeches and satires, sometimes proclaimed on their behalf by the bards, could make or break a chief's reputation. There were also doctors, of whom the MacBeths were the most highly regarded. An Irish poem quoted by Simms (2007) suggests that they might have accompanied armies on campaign, though the context implies that they were not expected to be successful in treating the terrible wounds inflicted by two-handed swords and axes: 'O grandson of Ruaidhri… it is no help to one you wound in the conflict to have a doctor in a house nearby.' Craftsmen in wood, iron and stone, who were classed like the poets and musicians as '*oes dana*', or 'men of art', enjoyed similar social status. They included the sculptors responsible for the hundreds of carved grave slabs in West Highland churchyards, which are among our best sources for the appearance of the men, ships and weapons of the era. The MacPhedrans of Benderloch near the mouth of Loch Linnhe, like the MacNabs of nearby Barachastlain, were among the hereditary families of blacksmiths who manufactured iron weapons and tools for the clans, though the local iron was not considered high enough quality for sword blades, which were mostly imported from Germany or Spain and fitted with locally made hilts.

Mobilisation, music and banners

In the seventeenth and eighteenth centuries, the fighting men of a clan were summoned by means of the '*crann tara*' or 'fiery cross', and it is usually assumed that a similar method was in use in our period. Duffy (2015) quotes the earl of Breadalbane, writing in 1744, who states that the cross was fixed onto a pole which was burnt (not necessarily burning) at one end, and dipped in blood at the other. This signified that anyone who refused the summons would not only suffer disgrace, but risked having his house burnt by his own chief. The custom was also common in Scandinavia, and may have been borrowed from the Vikings in earlier centuries. The cross was carried through the country by relays of runners, and in Breadalbane in 1745, it was said to have covered more than 30 miles in three hours (Dwelly, 1973). Numerous superstitions were involved in the ritual; for example, if the man who carried it met an armed warrior on the way, it was taken as a sign of good luck, but the first game animal encountered when the clan marched out had to be killed, while to meet a bare-footed woman was potentially bad luck, which had to be countered by drawing a drop of blood from her forehead with a dagger.

In this connection, it may be of interest to consider the means by which Highland armies actually traversed the country when on campaign. The clans of the Isles and the coastal districts would have travelled by sea when possible, but even the MacDonalds of the Isles were obliged to go by land when campaigning on the other side of the country in Easter Ross, for example, while clans such as the Mackays undertook the great majority of their expeditions overland. Unlike the Irish, the Scottish Highlanders did not fight on horseback, and the country bred few horses large enough to bear a man in armour. The fourteenth-century commentator Jean Froissart (quoted in Heath, 1982) describes Lowland armies as riding to battle on the small local ponies but then dismounting to fight, and it is possible that some of the clans of the eastern and central Highlands did likewise, but none of the sources for the campaigns described here actually record this practice. Horses were certainly bred in the Highlands, and John Major says that hundreds were regularly brought for sale to towns like Perth and Dundee, but in the west, where most of the clan conflicts took place, pasture for them was scarcer and of poorer quality and long-distance travel was undertaken mainly by sea. Some areas, like Major's 'Alps of Scotland' and the 'Rough Bounds' of the west coast, were regarded as so rough, mountainous and boggy that they were impassable to even the local horsemen. The warriors in our campaigns, therefore, would usually have marched as they fought, on foot.

Eighteenth-century English accounts are full of complaints about the lack of roads in the Highlands, and it is often stated that there were none at all before the British Army under General George Wade began their construction in the 1720s. This may be true as far as paved roads suitable for wheeled vehicles were concerned, and would explain why the heavy siege equipment that appears in accounts of the Wars of Independence seems not to have been employed north of Stirling. In fact, stretches of decent road may have existed, at least in the more accessible parts of the Highlands, where there was a powerful enough incentive to build and maintain them. Professor Barrow quotes an account of a road 'for carts to pass with wyne' that was apparently made in the thirteenth century between Atholl in Perthshire and Ruthven in Badenoch, or, in other words, over the bleak Pass of Drumochter along the route taken today by the A9 ('Land Routes', in Barrow, 1992). On the other hand, there was no incentive to build specifically military roads, as the clan armies had no need for wheeled vehicles. They travelled on foot and lived on oatmeal, which they carried on their persons, and milk from the herds that they brought with them or stole along the way. They needed no tents, as they were used to sleeping wrapped in their cloaks while herding their animals in their summer pastures. If the weather was wet or cold, the cloak or plaid could be dipped in a stream and then wrung out; this caused the fibres to swell and keep out wind or water more effectively – well worth the brief discomfort of wrapping oneself in damp cloth. Eighteenth-century accounts emphasise the mobility of Highland armies even in terrain that others would have regarded as impassable; they forded rivers, for example, by simply linking arms to prevent the men from being swept away and pushing through en masse, and the scouts or '*ghillies*' who preceded them prided themselves in being able to lead the army across any obstacle (Duffy, 2015). Duffy also quotes an eighteenth-century source that describes how the clan regiments in the Jacobite army of 1745 could travel 20 miles a day for up to four days, moving at a 'dog trot, or upon a half run'. By this time, however, armour had long ago been abandoned and all the warriors fought in effect like medieval *caterans*, so the mobility of clan armies might have been somewhat less in the days when the elite would be taking the field in heavy armour that, even if it was not worn until battle was imminent, would have had to be carried, either by its owner or by a retainer.

In the Middle Ages, marching and preparation for battle, like agricultural work and the rowing of ships, were probably accompanied by both improvised singing and instrumental music. The most prestigious instrument of the early medieval clans was the harp, and the epic poems of the bard or '*ollamh*', celebrating the deeds of warriors, were originally proclaimed to the accompaniment of the '*clarsach*', the traditional Celtic harp strung with brass wire. The Welsh chronicler Gerald de Barri mentions the skill of the Scottish harpists as early as the twelfth century, and John Major still regarded it as the typical Highland instrument when he was writing nearly 400 years later. Bardic compositions in praise of the chiefs and their warriors form a major part of medieval Gaelic literature and can be useful sources for our purposes, although of course they must be used with caution. Inevitably, they portray their subjects as they would have liked to see themselves, as mighty warriors and defenders of their people in the tradition of the legendary Irish heroes, and also as the bards would have liked them to be: a recurring theme in many of the poems is the lord's unstinting generosity to poets! The bards were not restricted to post-battle performances in castle or hall, but could also appear on the battlefield to inspire the troops before the clash of arms. We do not know how widespread this practice was, but the best-known example was at the Battle of Harlaw in 1411, when the MacDonald bard Lachlann Mor MacMhuirich performed his '*Brosnachadh Chatha*' or 'Call to Arms' before the Highland army. This work was preserved in the 'Red Book of Clanranald', an eighteenth-century manuscript attributed to Lachlann Mor's kinsman Niall MacMhuirich, and is still performed today (search 'The Harlaw Brosnachadh' on YouTube). Not to be confused with the 'Ballad of Harlaw', which is a sixteenth-century composition in Scots, the 'Brosnachadh' is an alliterative Gaelic poem that is almost impossible to translate, but it reminds its listeners of their supposed descent from Conn of the Hundred Battles, and incites them to acts of ferocity and daring worthy of the ancient heroes, beginning, 'Children of Conn remember, hardihood in time of battle'.

Once battle had begun, however, the notes of the harp and the voice of the poet would not have been easy to hear over the din, so neither was very suitable for transmitting orders in combat. Consequently, Jean de Froissart tells us that in the fourteenth century, Scottish warriors carried horns, which they would blow to communicate with each other or intimidate the enemy (Heath, 1982). Gary West (in Spiers et al, 2012) argues that the use of the bagpipes in war dates from around the beginning of the sixteenth century, and was linked to the need for a more effective instrument for controlling and inspiring troops in the inter-clan warfare that broke out after the suppression of the lordship of the Isles in 1493. Rixson cites a Mr John Knox, who visited the Highlands in the eighteenth century, as saying that the bagpipes were also played on board ships, which 'makes these poor people forget their toils'. The first explicit mention of bagpipes being used on the battlefield comes from a French observer at the Battle of Pinkie in 1547 (West, 2012), and an illustration in the 'Códice de Trajes', which shows an Irish soldier playing the pipes, is ascribed by the British Library website to the same year. However, it is one of the main arguments of the present book that there was a great deal of ferocious clan warfare before 1493, and although there is no definite proof, a number of arguments suggest that the pipes might have been used on the battlefield in some form well before the end of the fifteenth century. The instrument itself was certainly known; it had become popular among troubadours in Europe during the twelfth century, and within Scotland it is depicted in fourteenth-century carvings from

Melrose Abbey and Roslin Chapel, though admittedly not in a military context (West, 2012). Its adaptation to war probably depended on the evolution of the combination of tenor and bass drones, which produce a particularly powerful sound (Bingham, 1991). The West Highland Museum in Fort William has a set of bagpipes said to have been played at Bannockburn (1314), though their provenance is uncertain and they are probably of much later date. 'War pipes' of unspecified type are mentioned at the Battle of the North Inch in 1396, and the sixteenth-century anthology of poems known as the 'Bannatyne Manuscript' claims that MacLeod pipers played a crucial role at the Battle of Glendale, which was fought on Skye around 1513. When the MacDonald leader was killed and his head placed on a spear, the pipers were ordered to play a MacDonald lament in order to draw the enemy's attention to it; this psychological warfare was successful and the demoralised MacDonalds fled. Donald Campbell (1862) states, without citing any evidence, that Laclann Mor MacMhuirich lived to see the pipes replace the 'Brosnachadh', of which he was the master, and despised them on that account. Perhaps more persuasive is the argument that the '*Ceol mor*' or 'great music' of the bagpipes seems to emerge fully developed in the late sixteenth century, alongside the rise of famous pipers and composers like the MacCrimmons of Skye (Bingham). Although distinct from military music as such, a formal system of such uniqueness and complexity as the *Ceol mor* would seem to require a considerable period of development, which might well have begun with laments for the dead of the numerous wars of the fifteenth century.

The use of flags to identify the warring clans and their leaders is mentioned in several of the battle accounts cited here, but their exact form is seldom clear. Normal practice in feudal Europe was for the standard – a long, tapering flag with a rounded tail – to be flown in a static position to identify a camp or headquarters, while the square or rectangular banner was carried into battle to accompany a knight banneret or the equivalent, who in the Highlands would generally be the chief or sub-chief of a clan (Heath, 1982). There were of course many other types of flag designed as rallying points, or to identify the allegiance of an army or its constituent units, or even to invoke divine protection – for example the Scottish saltire or Saint Andrew's cross, which was displayed when fighting the English since 1385 at the latest, or the image of Saint Margaret carried by James IV's army at Flodden. It seems that even quite small Highland armies might be accompanied by an array of flags and banners, especially if they comprised contingents from more than one clan; the Clanranalds and their allies at Blar na Leine were seen to be flying no fewer than seven, or one for approximately every seventy men.

Most of the clan banners in use today date from a later period; only two supposed examples survive from the fifteenth century, and in both cases, their provenance is obscure. The Fairy Flag of the MacLeods of Dunvegan can still be seen at Dunvegan Castle, but the remains are fragmentary and have obviously been much patched over the centuries. Mackay (1924) relates the traditional MacLeod accounts of this flag, according to which it was a gift from the fairy wife of one of their chiefs and had the magical power to save the clan when unfurled at times of great peril. He also quotes Dr Norman MacLeod, who examined the remains of the flag in 1799 when the chest in which it was kept was broken open. At that time it 'consisted of a square piece of very rich silk, with crosses wrought with gold thread, and several elf spots stitched with great care on different parts of it'. It can still be seen on display at Dunvegan Castle, but the crosses are no longer visible and the 'elf spots' appear to be repairs made in red thread rather than part of the original pattern. The silk is now a shade of brownish yellow, but may have originally been cream or white. According to the Dunvegan Castle website (www.dunvegancastle.com), the material has been dated to between the fourth and seventh centuries AD, and probably originated in Syria or Rhodes. It quotes a Mr Wace at the Victoria and Albert Museum as suggesting that it may have been brought back from the Holy Land by the Norwegian king, Harald Hardrada, who was believed to have been an ancestor of the MacLeods. It is quite likely that it had some connection with the Crusades, in view of its apparent age and the crosses that once adorned it. The flag is said to have been flown at the battles of Bloody Bay (see Chapter 5) and Glendale, and even as late as the victory over the MacDonalds in 1578 known as the Spoiling of the Dyke, but it had evidently been relegated to a locked chest long before Norman MacLeod saw it. This was not the only example of a superstition being attached to some artefact that was believed to bring success in battle. Martin Martin refers to a green stone, about the size of a goose egg, which was still kept on the Isle of Arran in his day. It was said to have once belonged to a Saint Molingus, who had been a chaplain to the Lord of the Isles. The belief was that the MacDonald lords had always carried this stone into battle, and that if it was thrown into the midst of the enemy, they would all run away.

The second survival is the white banner of the Mackays, which is now in the National Museum of Scotland. Traditionally it was believed to have been carried by Iain Aberach Mackay at the Battle of Druim na Coub (Chapter 4) circa 1433, and remained in the possession of the clan standard-bearer until 1897 (Mackay, 1924). The Statistical Account of 1791 tends to confirm this story, as it mentions it as being in the custody of a member of the Aberach family at that date. There is no reason to doubt that the fifteenth-century Aberach Mackays did go into battle beneath a white flag, or that the traditional slogan of the clan – '*Am Bratach Bhan Chlann Aiodhe!*' or 'The White Banner of Clan Mackay!' – commemorates this fact. Unfortunately, it is unlikely that the present item is the original one (MacDougall, 1953). What is left of it is a rectangle of cream silk measuring about 30 inches by 16, which is much smaller than the usual dimensions of a battle flag. It bears the rather crudely worked image of a shield with a blue lion rampant on it, and above it what appears to be a fist surrounded by legends in Scots and Gaelic. The latter, '*Be Tren*' (*Biodh Treun*), means 'Be Valiant' in the Mackay dialect, and was also used as a war cry of the Strath Naver branch of the clan. At an unknown date, a leather strip has been added to one of the short sides, which is usually assumed to mark the hoist, but if so, the shield would have been on its side when the flag was flown. Two explanations have been offered for this anomaly; one is that what survives is only a remnant of a much larger flag, which would originally have had the hoist along what is now a long side. Alternatively, it might always have had roughly its current dimensions, in which case it would have hung vertically from a pole along the top. This is not the usual construction for war flags, but it is found in banners designed to hang on the wall of a building such as a church. The latter theory is the most likely, since MacDougall states that 'expert opinion' has dated the banner to the late sixteenth or early seventeenth century rather than the early fifteenth. A possible explanation is alluded to in an anonymous addendum to the account of Robert Mackay (1829), which mentions a tradition that the flag was nearly lost in a fight between the Aberachs and another branch of the clan which took place near Syre in Strath Naver sometime after 1579. It is possible that it really was lost or badly damaged, and the present one may have been embroidered as a replacement. In that case, it was probably never actually carried into battle, but it does imply that the flag that was flown at Druim na Coub would have been broadly similar in design. The arms of the chief of Clan Mackay in 1503, illustrated in Mackay (1906), display some similar themes, with three blue stars surmounted by a hand on a white field. The stars are also reminiscent of the flag of the earls of Sutherland, which from an early date has borne three yellow stars on a red field. Both are said by Robert Mackay (1829) to have been derived from the arms of the family of Moray or Murray.

The flags of the Lords of the Isles and their followers appear to have displayed a similar set of heraldic symbols, although much of our evidence dates from later than the period discussed here. Mackay (1924) quotes a description of the banner of the MacDonalds of Clanranald by the seventeenth-century Gaelic poet Iain Lom which mentions a castle, a salmon, a ship, a red hand, an eagle (inexplicably omitted from Mackay's English translation), a tree and a lion (red in the original, though the translation does not say so). He also cites verses by Lom's approximate contemporary Iain Dall Mackay, the

'Blind Piper of Gairloch', who refers to the ship, lion and red hand on the banner of the MacDonalds of Sleat. Most of these motifs are similar to the ones that appear quartered on the arms and heraldic banners of the clan chiefs today. The ship or galley was a device associated with the MacDonalds from an early date, although Robert Mackay alleged that it had been copied from an earlier and almost identical version used by the earls of Caithness. The salmon, which was associated with Somerled, the twelfth-century ancestor of the MacDonalds, also appeared on the flags of the MacLeans. The red eagle was borne along with the galley in the arms of the Lords of the Isles, as attested by the sixteenth-century herald Sir David Lyndsay (Laing, 1878), while the red lion has been featured on Scottish flags at least since the reign of William 'the Lion' in the late twelfth century. The red hand is most commonly associated nowadays with Ulster, but it was a popular motif in western Scotland in the Middle Ages, being borne by, among others, the MacLeans and the MacNeils of Barra. The flag of the Mackenzies, known as the '*caber feidh*' or the 'deer's antlers', which features a stag's head in gold on a blue ground, was said to have originated with a chief who saved the thirteenth-century King Alexander III from being gored by a stag, so many have been in use from around this time.

The chiefs and their close kin may have borne similar heraldic symbols on shields, but in the absence of uniforms, the rank and file warriors were usually distinguished from their enemies by a badge or field sign, which was often a sprig of a specific plant. In the seventeenth and eighteenth centuries, this was often worn in the bonnets that had then become fashionable, but in earlier times, when men either wore metal helmets or went bareheaded, it would probably have been attached to a spear shaft. For this purpose, the various branches of Clan Donald traditionally used heather, the Mackays reed or bulrush, the Sutherlands sedge, and the Mackenzies deer's grass or holly. The MacLeods of Lewis and Harris were associated respectively with the cowberry and juniper. Clans MacLean and Cameron both claim the crowberry as their badge, with, respectively, holly and oak as alternatives, perhaps introduced when they found themselves on opposite sides in one of the countless clan conflicts. The Frasers are known to have used yew in the late seventeenth century, and may have done so earlier; their traditional gathering place in the sixteenth century was at Tomnahurich, the 'Hill of Yews', near Inverness. These gathering places were where the clan warriors would muster when the call to arms was issued by their chiefs, and their names were often used as war cries, known as *Gaoir Chatha* or *Cath-ghairm*, designed to unite and inspire the men in battle. The *Cath-ghairm* was distinct from the '*Brosnachadh Chatha*' or 'Call to Arms', and also from the *Sluagh-ghairm* or rallying cry, the Gaelic word for which has given rise to the English word slogan (Fraser, 1953). Some of the best-known rallying cries, like the clan mottos that appeared on the crests of their chiefs, were either too long to have been useful as war cries, or in Latin, French or English and so incomprehensible to the rank and file. So despite the romantic tradition, the Camerons of Lochiel did not go into battle shouting '*Chlanna nan con, thigibh a so 's gheibh sibh feoil!*', or 'Sons of dogs, come here and get flesh!' That was a rallying cry, but their war cry was '*Da thaobh Lochiall 's da thaobh Lochaidh – Lochiall! Lochiall!*', 'Both sides of Lochiel and both sides of Loch Lochy – Lochiel! Lochiel!' (Fraser, 1953). Other famous war cries date from long after our period. For example, the MacLeans' '*Fear eil 'airson Eachainn!*', 'Another for Hector!', commemorates the battle of Inverkeithing in 1651, when seven brothers are said to have died protecting their chief, Sir Hector of Duart. The official heraldic motto of the MacDonalds was '*Per Mare per Terras*', 'By Sea and by Land', but when going into action they would shout, '*Fraoch Eilean!*', 'Heather Isle!', and the Campbells yelled, '*Cruachan!*' the name of the mountain overlooking Loch Awe. The Mackenzies had '*Tulach Ard!*', 'The Hill of Alarm', which was the site of a warning beacon near their castle of Eilean Donan, and their MacRae allies had '*Sgurr Fhuaran!*', one of the mountains known as the Five Sisters of Kintail. The cry of the Frasers of Lovat, '*A' Mhorfhaich!*', 'The Sea Field', referred to their stronghold at Lovat, on the shore of the Beauly Firth.

Chapter 3

Dress, Weapons and Armour of the Clan Wars

Costume and armour: change and continuity

By the late fifteenth century, several of what were later to become the iconic elements of Highland culture were beginning to make their appearance; the first mention of whisky distilling dates from 1495, and the use of the bagpipes in war is attested from soon after that. However, the men who fought in the battles discussed here would have looked very different from their more familiar descendants of the seventeenth and eighteenth centuries in their tartan plaids and blue bonnets. The costume most typically associated with the latter, the belted plaid, was not yet in existence. It seems to have been a fashion that appeared among Scottish soldiers fighting in Ireland in the late sixteenth century, and so in our period we should imagine warriors still looking more like Vikings than the typical image of Highlanders. What Martin Martin calls 'the first habit worn by persons of distinction' was the '*leine croich*' or 'saffron shirt', a voluminous garment made from up to twenty-four ells of cloth (the Scottish ell being roughly equivalent to a metre), which reached as far as the knees, and swathed the upper body in what Bishop Leslie of Ross, writing around 1578, calls 'numerous folds and wide sleeves' (Leslie, 1830). 'The rich', says Leslie, coloured these shirts yellow with saffron, while those unable to afford this expensive dye preserved theirs from the weather by smearing them with grease. Despite Martin's remark about 'persons of distinction', the yellow *leine croich* is frequently illustrated in sixteenth-century sources, such as the German costume book known as the 'Códice de Trajes', now in the Biblioteca National de España, being worn by ordinary lightly armed men lacking any armour or sign of rank. It was probably more of a fashion item, worn by anyone who could afford it, than a form of rank insignia. Nevertheless, the appearance of the shirt (and especially its colour) might give an important clue to the status of the wearer. Reid (2013) refers to the death of Angus Mackintosh, chief of Clan Chattan, who was shot dead at the siege of Ruthven Castle in 1592 by a musketeer who identified him by his 'yellow war coat'. It may not be coincidence that, according to Martin, the *leine croich* was abandoned around this time, although Reid mentions the cutting off of the supply of saffron dye from Ireland by the Elizabethan conquest as a more likely cause.

Over the shirt would normally be worn a cloak, or mantle, either of one colour or several. Leslie says that the rich preferred multi-coloured garments, but those of the poorer people were plain. George Buchanan, writing in the late sixteenth century (quoted in Reid, 2013), says that stripes in blue and purple were once the most popular, but that by the time he wrote, they had been superseded by plain brown, which provided better concealment among the heather. This preference for camouflage over display might be attributable, like the disappearance of the yellow shirt, to the spread of firearms. By the end of the seventeenth century, Martin Martin was describing plaids in different colours and patterns according to the wearer's place of origin, a custom that eventually developed into the nineteenth-century idea of clan tartans, but there is no evidence from our period that any such formal system existed, or even that the patterns used necessarily resembled what we now know as tartan. Men who did not wear a helmet into battle generally went bareheaded, the iconic blue bonnet being a Lowland fashion adopted by the Highlanders in the seventeenth century (Cannan, 2009).

By the fifteenth century, the characteristic armour of the Highland warrior was beginning to look distinctly old fashioned. It is clear both from written accounts and from contemporary depictions, such as the early sixteenth-century figures carved on the tombs of the MacLeod chiefs in St Clement's Church at Rodel on the island of Harris, that the coats of mail and open-faced helmets that had typified European warriors of the early Middle Ages were still in widespread use. Quilted protective coats, or aketons, which were probably designed originally for wearing underneath mail, were also worn on their own as the principal defence, as is shown on the tomb carvings of Gilbride Mackinnon on Iona and Donald MacGillespie from Finlaggan, among many others. (There are good illustrations of these, as well as the Rodel figures, in Caldwell, 2007.) These are presumably the garments that John Major refers to in his well-known description of 'the common folk among the Wild Scots', who 'go out to battle with the whole body clad in a linen garment sewed together in patchwork, well daubed with wax or with pitch, and with an over-coat of deerskin'. A story quoted by Alexander Mackenzie (1894) alleges that at the Battle of Bealach nam Brog (the Pass of the Shoes) in 1452, men took off their shoes and tied them to their belts as a defence against arrows. This tale is likely to have been concocted later in an attempt to explain the name given to the battle, but it suggests an awareness that some poorer men might have had to go into combat without adequate protection. The better equipped warriors, Major adds, 'cover the whole body with a coat of mail, made of iron rings'. In fact, it seems likely that the mail coat would usually have been worn on top of the aketon by those who could afford it, rather than as a substitute, if only because without some sort of padding underneath it, mail would be not only very uncomfortable to wear but potentially dangerous, as the rings could be driven into the wearer's flesh by a crushing blow. This is not confirmed by any written descriptions contemporary with the battles discussed here, but Bishop Leslie, writing in the 1570s, describes the Highlanders of his day as wearing a coat of mail 'over a leather jerkin… which we call an acton'. The carving on the tomb of Alexander MacLeod at Rodel also appears to show this combination of mail and padded or quilted armour. Perhaps, as Caldwell suggests, there were aketons designed to be worn on their own as well as thinner and lighter versions for use under mail. It is noteworthy that this style of equipment was in effect the same as that which had been prescribed by a decree of Robert the Bruce in 1318 (Cannan, 2009): an aketon or coat of mail, and a bascinet or open-faced helmet. Bruce's laws had applied to all Scots with an annual income of ten pounds or more, but by the time that Major wrote at the beginning of the sixteenth century, Lowland warriors had largely adopted the textile coats with integral metal plates which were known as jacks, and mail had come to be associated specifically with the Highlanders. Some of the richer men surely possessed items of the more up-to-date plate armour that was adopted in the rest of western Europe during the fourteenth century, as it is often illustrated on grave slabs (Heath, 1982), but to judge from the lack of any mention of it being worn in battle, it seems that plate would have been in very short supply, and perhaps worn only for ceremonial purposes. In most of Europe from the fourteenth century onwards, a visor was frequently added to the bascinet to protect the wearer's face, but like the plate body armour, this was seldom seen in the Highlands. However, a story related by Donald Sage (1889) and attributed to the year 1511 tells how the chief of Clan Keith was entertained in the Caithness stronghold of his enemies, the Gunns, but remained unrecognised until he removed his 'vizor'. After the ensuing fight, he was pursued to Dirlot in Sutherland and shot in the face with an arrow while 'wearing his helmet, but with the vizor unclosed'. As the visor plays such a central role in the story, it is unlikely to be a later addition, but it may have been remembered because it was unusual. The Keiths were in any case relative newcomers to Caithness, and so were perhaps more influenced by Lowland fashions than the clans further west.

The reluctance of the latter to adopt new equipment has sometimes been ascribed to cultural conservatism or to the relative poverty of the clansmen, who were obliged to re-use equipment inherited from their ancestors, but neither of these theories is very satisfactory. It will be evident from the campaign narratives that follow that Highland chiefs were frequent – if not always voluntary – visitors to the royal court at Edinburgh, where they must have become familiar with modern innovations such as plate armour. As for their supposed poverty,

John Major describes the rank and file of the 'Wild Scots' as better equipped than their equivalents among the Lowlanders (and indeed the English), who went into battle wearing only woollen clothing. In fact, there are some compelling reasons why the Highlanders may have consciously chosen to retain their old styles of armour. The first is mobility. In contrast to the situation in Ireland, where the upper classes provided some effective light cavalry, everyone in a Highland army – of whatever rank – was expected to fight on foot even if they rode to the battlefield beforehand, and a textile aketon would certainly have been lighter than metal armour and so more suitable for rapid movement over the rough and often boggy terrain. 'Their whole armour was light', says Bishop Leslie, 'that they might more easily slip from their enemies' hands if they chanced to fall into such a strait.' Mail, although heavier than the aketon, was also more flexible than plate, even though a near ankle-length coat such as is described by George Buchanan and illustrated at Rodel would hardly have been easy to run in. On the other hand, plate armour did not necessarily provide very good protection against the heavy two-handed swords and axes that were popular in the Highlands, and which could knock a man down and leave him vulnerable even if his armour successfully withstood the blow. A combination of mail and padded undergarment might in this case be just as effective in preventing serious injury. Where plate was unquestionably superior was against arrows (Stretton, 2018), and we shall see in Chapter 8 how the plate-armoured Lowland nobility at the Battle of Flodden withstood the English archery much better than the Highlanders, but in internal clan warfare, where archery was mainly preliminary to the decisive hand-to-hand combat, and the sort of specialist armour-piercing arrowheads found in contemporary England seem not to have been used, this advantage might not have been regarded as worth the penalties. Most importantly, perhaps, a mail coat was significantly easier to put on than plate and, crucially, to take off in a hurry. Plate protection was made up of a number of pieces that all needed to be fitted separately and laced together, usually with the help of a squire or page. A mail coat, by contrast, was a one-piece garment which, although awkward to put on unassisted because of its flexible and 'slippery' construction, could be removed fairly easily just by bending forward, extending the arms and allowing it to fall under its own weight. (There is a good discussion of this procedure in Hill & Freiberg, 2015.) As discussed in Chapter 2, the worst slaughter in medieval battles often took place when a defeated army tried to flee across an obstacle such as a stream or bog; this was actually one of the main causes of the greatest ever loss of life on a British battlefield, at Towton in Yorkshire in 1461, during the Wars of the Roses. In such a situation, being able to dispose of armour in order to escape more quickly could have made the difference between life and death, leading to the paradoxical situation that in certain circumstances, heavier protection might increase rather than reduce the wearer's vulnerability. This may even be one reason for what seems to have been a relatively low death rate in battle among defeated Highland leaders compared to that among English noblemen in the wars of the fifteenth century. Possibly for the same reason, their vulnerability to archery notwithstanding, a significant number of Highlanders of rank escaped from the disaster at Flodden, which claimed the lives of so many of their Lowland counterparts. Furthermore, we know from eighteenth-century accounts that Highland warriors were very suspicious of leaders who did not speak their language or share their traditional attire, which was perhaps a consequence of the clan ideology that emphasised their descent from a common ancestor. So, even if a chief had been able to afford the most modern protection, he might have been reluctant to wear it in battle for fear of seeming to be unduly concerned for his own safety, and so damaging his reputation among his followers.

David Caldwell has speculated that another reason for the continuing popularity of padded cotton armour might have been its value as a warm and waterproof garment for use at sea. He suggests that further research should be carried out to establish whether a 'cotun' waterproofed with wax or pitch would have been buoyant enough to act as a sort of life jacket for a man in the water. I am not aware that any such research has been attempted, but the idea seems very plausible. It is less certain whether such buoyancy would be enough to counteract the extra weight of a coat of mail, and 'living history' experiments along these lines might be inadvisable for health and safety reasons!

Close-combat weapons

By the middle of the sixteenth century, the two-handed sword had become the most prominent close-quarters weapon in descriptions of Highland soldiers and their battles, and so it would clearly be of interest for our purposes to establish when it first came into use. Of course, many medieval swords were capable of being used in either one hand or two, but by Neil Melville's definition (Melville, 2018) the true two-hander is long and heavy enough to require both hands to wield it effectively, and has a hilt long enough for the hands to be spaced at least a foot (30cm) apart. This enables the user to pivot the blade using the leading hand as a fulcrum, a method that enables accurate and powerful cuts to be made very rapidly despite the size of the weapon. It also prevents him from using a shield to protect himself against incoming blows, so that the sword has to be employed simultaneously for offence and defence. The fighting style and the whole approach to combat was therefore very different when using a two-handed weapon, making the question of when and how it was introduced to the Highlands of more than technical interest. In Europe, the fourteenth century saw the appearance of some very large swords, which were basically scaled-up versions of the earlier one-handed 'great sword', and appear to have been ceremonial items rather than intended for combat. Several examples, ascribed to the reigns of Edward III and Henry IV of England, can be seen in St George's Chapel, Windsor, and in the Tower of London. The famous sword said to have belonged to William Wallace (died 1305), which is on show at the Wallace Monument near Stirling, has no proven connection with Wallace and appears to be a composite of several much later weapons. But the earliest indisputable evidence of a weapon fitting the above definition of a combat two-handed sword seems to be from the now lost tombstone of Reinier de Valkenburg in Limburg, Belgium, who died in 1342 (Melville, 2018). The new weapon may have spread fairly quickly to Scotland, as less than four decades later, in 1378, Froissart describes the Scottish knight Sir Archibald Douglas as wielding a sword 'two ells long' (about 6 feet or 2 metres), which other men could scarcely lift. Melville also cites a grave slab from Foveran in Aberdeenshire, which carries the images of two knights who are thought to have been killed at the Battle of Harlaw in 1411. This identification is based only on stylistic similarities with the effigy at Kinkell, near Inverurie, of Sir Gilbert de Greenlaw, who is known to have died in the same battle, but the armour shown is certainly from the right period. Each man is holding a very large sword diagonally in front of him, with its tip apparently resting on the ground and the pommel roughly level with his shoulder. The hilts are not as long as was usual for true two-handers, but if the weapons are to scale, they could hardly have been wielded in any other way. If this is indeed the earliest pictorial evidence for the weapon in Scotland, it neatly corroborates James Fraser's claim (Fraser, 1905) that a two-handed sword was used in the defence of Inverness in the same campaign.

It is therefore highly likely that two-handed swords of some description were already in use in Scotland at the beginning of our period, even if they had not yet attained the iconic form of the sixteenth-century Highland two-hander, with its long hilt and forward-swept quillons. These weapons may have been adopted with exceptional enthusiasm because they fitted into the existing fighting ethos of the Highlands and Islands, where individual single combat was traditional and the tactically similar Viking axe was already familiar, just as the two-hander no doubt reinforced the emphasis on individual heroics in battle. Elsewhere in Europe, the two-handed sword fell out of favour during the early sixteenth century, reverting largely to its original ceremonial function, but it continued as the characteristic weapon of the Scottish Highlander until it was banned by the government along with bows and firearms as a symbol of lawlessness in the early seventeenth century. The clans then reverted to the use of the single-handed sword, the famous 'claymore' of the Jacobite rebellions, but there is no reason to suppose that single-handers were not in use throughout our period, either as a backup for men armed with spears or axes, or as the primary weapon in conjunction with a shield. As can be seen from numerous carved grave slabs from medieval Highland churchyards (see Plate 2), the designs of these swords were little different from their contemporaries in the rest of Europe, with the iconic basket-hilted two-edged broadsword probably appearing in the mid- to late sixteenth century. Before that, the most common type was what was called in English a longsword, which Neil Grant (2020) defines as a dual-purpose cut-and-thrust weapon, similar in length and weight to other single-handed swords of the time, but with a longer hilt, enabling it to be wielded in either one or two hands. For this reason, it was known in Scots as a 'halflang'. A long single-edged knife or dirk is often mentioned being carried as a sidearm by men wielding swords or bows. According to an eighteenth-century observer, this was not so much an everyday utensil as 'a concealed weapon, hid under the plaid for secret stabbing, and, in a close encounter, there is no defence against it' (quoted in Duffy, 2015).

The word 'claymore', incidentally, has caused confusion at least since the days of Samuel Johnson (1775), who in his account of his tour of the Western Isles refers to 'the glaymore, or great two-handed sword', which had been used there 'anciently', but had by then been replaced by 'the two-edged sword and target, or buckler'. However, Johnson admitted to knowing no Gaelic and was entirely ignorant of the existence of any medieval literature in that language, so he would not have known that the term 'claymore' was not in fact ancient. It derives from the Gaelic '*claidheamh mor*', which means, literally, 'great sword', but Melville states that the first attested use was in 1715, when it referred to the basket-hilted broadsword. He further argues that there are no literary references in Gaelic from the days when the two-hander was in use, so we cannot be sure what the men who wielded it called it in their own language. However, Donald Campbell (1862) quotes a verse from the poet William Ross that refers to a '*claidheamh da laimh*', which literally means a two-handed sword. Ross wrote in the late eighteenth century so he may not be a reliable guide to medieval terminology, but the Gaelic language was fairly conservative and there would have been little point in introducing a new word once the two-hander had gone out of use, so this may be the best available guess.

At least until the end of the fifteenth century, however, the most popular close-combat weapon, as it had been throughout the Middle Ages, was still the Norse style battle axe, the '*tuagh catha*'. The shafts of these weapons seem to have increased in length over the centuries so that they were now almost always wielded two-handed. There was no standard design for the axe head; some resembled their Viking predecessors, with a curved cutting edge and two equal sized 'horns' or curved projections at top and bottom, but by the sixteenth century, the edge was often straight and the upper horn of the axe head elongated into a point that could be used for thrusting, making the weapon the equivalent of a halberd rather than a traditional axe. Cannan (2010) illustrates several axe heads of both types that have been excavated in Ireland, and in view of the close connections between the two countries it is quite likely that both were also in widespread use in the clan wars of Scotland. John Major, in his account of the Battle of Bannockburn, describes the weapon of the Wild Scots as 'a two-edged battle axe, equally sharp on both sides', but it is not clear what he means by this. Medieval axes and halberds sometimes possessed a small spike or hammer opposite the blade, though this is not a feature associated with carvings or archaeological finds of Highland or Irish weapons. A double-headed axe, with a blade of similar weight on each side of the shaft, would be an unbalanced and most impractical weapon, but if the upper horn or projection of an axe head were sharpened on the back it might turn it into a useful thrusting weapon as well as allowing for effective reverse cuts. Major also mentions the 'double axe of Leith', which he says is 'much the same as the French halberd', and the Lochaber axe, which is 'single edged only', but is described as particularly deadly: 'Its course is lined by many a corpse, and death's pale face is constant there.' The Lochaber axe is well documented from the seventeenth century, and there is a good collection of the iron heads in the West Highland Museum in Fort William. They have a cutting edge which was fixed to the end of a long shaft, topped by a hook which would be useful for pulling a cavalryman off his horse, or perhaps for entangling the long flowing sleeves of the '*leine croich*'. The first contemporary mention of this weapon is in 1501, when James IV ordered an axe to be made 'of Lochabirt fasoun' (Cannan, 2009). Irish poetry describes the gallowglass axe as a precious possession, its head sometimes decorated with inscriptions in the ancient Ogham script. Some verses in praise of the MacSweeneys quoted by Simms (2007) imply that these inscriptions might even have been regarded as having magical powers: 'During the battle the man at Domhnall's side has little to apprehend, an ogham inscription is on his axe whose bounty is victory': 'You win command of every fight with your poison-charmed brown-based weapon'.

It is obvious that powerful weapons of this sort could not be used effectively without practice and training, and we occasionally hear of leaders who made a point of insisting on this (for example, Hugh Fraser of Lovat, for whom see Chapter 11). Major, in the account of the Wild Scots quoted above, adds that 'hardly would any weapons make stand against their axes handled as they knew to handle them'. But we know very little about exactly how swords and axes were used in combat. Short (2009) and Scott Thompson (2018) have reconstructed a series of drills for both weapons that would appear to be practical and effective, but both admit that they are speculative, being based on moves illustrated in medieval German manuals, combined with later drills for the one-handed broadsword and the practical experience of modern re-enactors. They include conventional cuts and parries together with striking with the sword hilt or the butt of the axe, and techniques for hooking an opponent's weapon or body with the axe head. The overall impression is that the axe, despite its less sophisticated construction, was just as effective, and required just as much skill to use properly, as the sword.

The spear had always been the primary weapon of Lowland Scots, and the 'schiltron' of close-packed spearmen was the main architect of victory over the English knights at Stirling Bridge and Bannockburn, but it seldom appears in Highland battle accounts in our era. It is nevertheless likely that it continued in use, and it appears in many of the effigies of warriors carved on fourteenth-century West Highland grave slabs (Heath, 1982). The heroes of Gaelic poetry often threw their spears from a distance, and there is no reason to suppose that the more lightly equipped *caterans* did not continue to do so, as the Irish kerns certainly did (Cannan, 2010). Scott Thompson quotes an account from 1583 which says that the Scots living north of the Grampian mountains employed bows 'and some darts, which they throw with great dexterity'. The more usual Scottish practice, however, was to hold the shaft in one or both hands and thrust, as was done at Bannockburn. Lowland spear shafts were normally around 12 to 14 feet in length, though fifteenth-century Acts of Parliament regularly tried to prescribe longer ones (Heath), but the versions illustrated on the grave slabs are shorter. This may be for artistic reasons, but Fergus Cannan (2009) suggests 8 feet as the length of a typical Highland spear. This would make it more practical for throwing, but also handier if kept in the hand for single combat, especially in a confined space such as on board a ship.

Fourteenth-century grave slabs often show men carrying flat-topped shields of the classic medieval type known today as 'heaters', but it is difficult to establish how common they still were. David Caldwell (2007) argues that the heater design was retained in sculpture, as it was a convenient shape for displaying heraldic charges, but that by the fifteenth century such shields were not actually used in battle. Instead, documents of the time refer only to the circular varieties known as targets and bucklers. Both were made of wood covered with leather, but the latter was a smaller version of the former, designed to be held in the left hand rather than strapped to the arm and so more suitable for an active defence. Lighter wicker versions were popular in Ireland, but apparently less so in Scotland. Caldwell, citing Acts of Parliament of 1456 and 1481, says that the target was specifically associated with the axe and the buckler with the sword, though he admits that the Highlanders ignored other legislation regarding armament, such as that ordering the adoption of the 18-foot pike in 1471, so this may not be reliable evidence for practice in all parts of the country. The Carlisle Charter of 1316 (illustrated in Reid, 2013) shows a man armed with a heater shield and single-handed axe and another who appears to be combining such a shield with a spear, so we can be fairly confident that this design was still in use for combat in the early fourteenth century, though we cannot be sure that the figures depicted are meant to represent Highlanders. Scott Thompson (2018), relying on the same evidence as that cited by Caldwell, reaches a different conclusion – that the heater shields were likely to be carried by men of higher rank than those who used targets and bucklers. Despite the lightly armed appearance of the Carlisle figures, this is supported by the fact that the grave figures associated with the heater types tend to be depicted in armour, and of course, they were likely to have been of high status if they possessed heraldic charges to display. In fact, by the fifteenth century we seldom hear of shields being used in battle by Highlanders at all. Men armed with two-handed weapons such as swords, axes or bows would not have been able to make effective use of a shield while doing so and so they may not have bothered to carry them, though Caldwell mentions that warriors in Ireland are known to have slung them on their backs while their hands were occupied.

Highland archery

Hand-held firearms were known in Scotland as early as the late fifteenth century, and as early as 1510, James IV installed craftsmen from the continent to manufacture them in Edinburgh (Cannan, 2009), but we do not hear of their appearance in any of the clan battles discussed here. In 1545, the Irish Privy Council reported to Henry VIII of England that the Hebridean soldiers who followed Donald Dubh to Ireland possessed 'few guns' (Rixson), which implies that they did have some. It is not known what sort of weapons they were, though they were probably handguns, as their galleys were too light to mount cannon. However, most Highlanders remained so unfamiliar with gunpowder weapons that at Haddington in 1548, according to the French observer Jean de Beaugué, they 'shut their ears and threw themselves on their bellies' every time the cannons fired. The principal missile weapon of the clans was still the bow, and this would continue to be the case until well into the seventeenth century. We have several sixteenth-century descriptions of Highland warriors armed with both bow and two-handed sword, a combination that set them apart from the Lowlanders with their long spears. Robert Lindesay of Pitscottie (1814), for example, tells how at the Battle of Flodden in 1513, the earl of Huntly's Highlanders 'with their bowis and tua handed swords' defeated the English billmen opposite them. The same source refers to the contingent of MacLean of Duart as armed with bows and 'halflangs'. Like the English longbow, the Highland bow was usually made of yew, and Mackay (1924) quotes a Gaelic poem that lists the materials needed for the ideal bow and arrows: 'Bow of yew from Easragain, eagle feather from Loch Treig, yellow wax from Galway town, arrowhead from MacPhedran.' Another version mentions arrows made of birch wood from Glen Orchy. It is interesting to note that most of the places mentioned are in the same region of the south-west Highlands: Easragain is on the north shore of Loch Etive in Argyllshire, while Glen Orchy runs roughly parallel to Loch Etive a few miles to the east, and Loch Treig is less than 20 miles away in the hills of Lochaber.

Fergus Cannan's argument that Scottish bows and archery techniques were inferior to those of the English has been discussed in my previous book. Scottish bows were cheaper than English longbows (Caldwell, 2012), which might imply that they were slightly shorter, but this need not mean that they were less powerful. Heath (1982) quotes a late fourteenth-century observer, Juan de Perelhos, as saying that although Irish bows were only half the length of English ones, they shot just as far. Where the Highland archers may have been at a disadvantage in an age of increasingly heavy armour was in the design of their arrowheads. These were mostly 'hooked', as George Buchanan (quoted in Cannan, 2010) puts it, or in other words, barbed broadheads intended for hunting, rather than the specialised armour-piercing varieties favoured for war – and manufactured in industrial quantities – in England. Mike Loades (2019) points out that different arrowheads were optimised for use against different types of target; the barbed types would cause massive blood loss to an unarmoured victim, whether man or deer, but would be less effective against armour, though Loades is perhaps overstating his case when he says that they were 'of no use against any type of metal armour', and of course the open-faced helmets and bare legs favoured by the Highlanders meant that even an armoured man still exposed plenty of unprotected areas that could be attacked. Donald Gorm MacDonald was killed in 1539 by just such a barbed arrow, which struck him in the knee (Chapter 11). The style of armour-piercing arrowhead favoured in fifteenth-century England was the short, solid 'bodkin' designed for smashing through plate, but Loades reports that in modern tests these failed to penetrate a combination of mail and textile armour covered with deerskin such as John Major describes. There were also long, needle-shaped arrowheads that would be better suited to penetrating between the rings of mail armour or cutting through thick padded aketons to reach the flesh behind them, but would bend and ricochet if they hit a hard surface such as a steel breastplate (Stretton, 2018). It would seem that these 'long bodkins' might have been very useful to the Highland archers in inter-clan battles, where mail and cotton padding were the most common forms of armour encountered, but we do not hear of them in battle accounts.

It is also worth mentioning that a number of modern commentators have argued that the effectiveness of an arrow against an armoured man might not necessarily have been dependent on whether or not his armour was penetrated. Loades discusses the debilitating effect on a man of being hit repeatedly by missiles which, although they did not reach his flesh, delivered heavy concussive blows to his head and body, potentially causing injury by blunt force trauma. Mark Stretton attempts to quantify this effect, calculating the energy delivered to a target by a particularly heavy arrow that he shot himself to have been 152.6 joules, compared to the 80 joules required to stop a human heart! He implies that death from this cause could have been a significant result of the use of heavy bows in warfare. Similar statistics have often been repeated in recent discussions of historical archery, and it is worth considering them in more detail because the implications for battlefield tactics are profound. Can it be true that an arrow could strike dead an armoured man just by hitting him, regardless of any protection offered by his armour? If so, would this not apply to a blow delivered by any other weapon, such as a sword or axe wielded in the hand? And if archery was particularly deadly for this reason, why was it not more decisive in the battles that we are discussing? In fact, the original source for the figure of 80 joules is not clear, and many other reports can be found to contradict it. According to the Northern Ireland Human Rights Commission ('Baton Rounds, A Review of the Human Rights Implications', Belfast, 2003), the British Army's L5A7 and L21A1 baton rounds or plastic bullets, as used for riot control in Belfast in the 1990s and early 2000s, had a kinetic energy of around 200 joules at a range of 50 meters, but although they have been responsible for numerous injuries, including broken bones and trauma to the chest, fatalities from cardiac arrest seem not to have been recorded. This is despite the fact that the victims were not wearing any sort of body armour. There is extensive medical literature on the phenomenon known as 'commotio cordis', which seems nowadays to be regarded mainly as a sports injury, involving sudden cardiac arrest as a result of impact by a cricket ball, hockey stick or similar object. Tragically, deaths do occur but they are uncommon, which is not surprising, as the fatal impact needs to be exactly perpendicular to the chest and to occur during a small fraction of the heart's cycle. Several mitigating factors would in any case reduce the amount of energy delivered by the majority of arrows. Mark Stretton was using a bow with a draw weight of 140 pounds, which is about twice the weight of what an average archer can manage, and shooting at very close range against a target that was positioned to minimise the likelihood of arrows glancing off or breaking. In battle, the targets would be at variable ranges, in motion and generally presenting themselves at an angle to the shooter, all of which would reduce the energy that they would absorb from a hit. The padded protection worn under armour would also dissipate some if not all of that energy. So any casualties caused by blunt force trauma would surely have been rare, and might be regarded more as freak accidents than as the outcome of an opponent's tactics. Archery could disorder and confuse an enemy, pick off individual leaders and wear down morale with a steady trickle of casualties, but Highland battles were always decided in the end in hand-to hand-fighting.

Nevertheless, the idea that Highland archery was ineffective was not shared by contemporaries, as is witnessed by the high status accorded to skilled bowmen and the numerous tales of feats of archery, reminiscent of those of Robin Hood but slightly better documented, which have been preserved. Donald Balloch's victory at Inverlochy in 1431 was attributed to his picked bowmen, and as discussed in Chapter 7, archery seems to have played an important part in the Mackenzie victory at Blar na Parc. The latter case involved the MacRaes, a small clan from Kintail that had a well-deserved reputation for skill with the bow, and John Dixon (1886) relates several stories of the ability of the archers of Kintail to hit targets at extraordinary ranges. In one of these, a party of MacLeods from Skye took a galley for a raid on the MacRaes living on the mainland near Gairloch. (This took place after the MacLeods had been expelled from the mainland by the Mackenzies, so probably sometime in the 1570s.) Approaching by night, they tied up the ship on a small island named Fraoch Eilean, or 'Heather Island', to wait for morning before launching their attack. But they had been spotted by the MacRaes, and two of the latter's best archers, the brothers Domhull and Iain MacIain Leith, were in position before dawn in the shelter of a rock on the mainland opposite the island, at a place that became known as Leachd nan Saighead, or the 'Stone of the Arrows'. Dixon says that the spot where they stood was still pointed out to visitors when he wrote. As soon as the light was good enough, the MacRaes started picking off the MacLeods, who at first could not even see their assailants. One of the ship's crew climbed the mast to get a better view, but Iain pinned him to the mast with an arrow. The MacLeods then cut the mooring rope and fled, but only two of them succeeded in getting home alive. They were said to have been so panic-stricken that they left their dead behind on the island. Fraoch Eilean in Loch Gairloch is marked on the modern OS Landranger map (grid reference NG797738), and assuming that it is the place referred to here, the shortest distance from the mainland is around 300 metres, which would be an extremely long range for a bowshot. Dixon says that the brothers' targets were 'nearly four hundred yards away'. It is perhaps not quite impossible for a lucky shot to hit a man at such a distance, but the arrow would not be likely to have sufficient penetrating power to transfix him and nail him to a wooden mast. Such feats are common in folklore, but it seems more reasonable to suppose that the brothers might simply have shot close enough to the island for their enemies to realise that they had been spotted and decide to retire. They would still have saved their people from a nasty raid, and can hardly be blamed if they had embellished the story of their exploit a little. Another story from Dixon seems to be an even more exaggerated version of this one, as it has Iain's brother Domhull hitting a MacLeod lookout on top of a mast at a distance of around half a mile, a feat that would be considered extraordinary even with a modern rifle. Mike Loades suggests 'approaching 300yd' as extreme range for a war arrow, and quotes Sir John Smythe, writing in 1590, as saying that although there were archers who could shoot light flight arrows to a range of twenty-four score or 480 yards, it would be futile to try to engage an enemy with volleys even at eighteen score, or 360 yards.

A seventeenth-century Cameron tradition further illustrates the pride that the Highlanders took in their archery (Drummond, 1842). A clansman had struck an Englishman with an arrow from a great distance, but the arrow did not penetrate far enough to kill him. Seeing this, the Cameron chief called out that the shot must have come from a weak arm, at which the offended warrior rushed into the midst of the enemy, pulled out the arrow and stuck it back into the victim's body as far as the feathers. Most Highlanders probably learned to shoot by hunting deer, but formal training in archery may have been more widespread than the records indicate. Scott Thompson (2018) quotes a nineteenth-century source that mentions a family of hereditary bowmen to the chief of Clan MacKinnon, whose duties included instructing the clansmen in the use of the bow. King James I was a great advocate of the bow, and in 1424 the Scottish parliament passed a law requiring men to practise shooting – and, famously, banning football, which was blamed for distracting them from their archery. However, James's inspiration was not his native Highlanders but the English longbow, which he had seen in action while accompanying English forces in France (Strickland & Hardy, 2005). In the early fifteenth century, Scottish Lowland archers served with distinction in France against the English, but after James's death, as Walter Bower lamented, nearly everyone gave up their bows and reverted to their traditional spears.

The cult of single combat

John Major seems to have believed that Highland battles never involved elaborate tactics, but were decided simply by a large number of individual combats. An encounter that he ascribes to the year 1431, and which may be intended to refer to Druim na Coub (Chapter 4), was, he says, fought between two equal forces numbering 1,200 '*caterans*' a side, who engaged in 'an equal number of duels' or single combats, with each man either slaying his opponent or being killed himself. This allegedly accounted for the very high casualty rate, as 'on both sides scarce one escaped with his life' – a claim originally made by Bower. However, it is not clear what Major's source was for this account of single combat, and it is possible that he simply assumed that that was how the unsophisticated Wild Scots fought. Elsewhere, he was forthright in condemning 'conflicts between two persons, such as are called duels', and included under this heading encounters between individual Scottish and English knights on the field of battle, as well as all forms of trial by combat. In this context, the Battle of the North Inch, fought at Perth in 1396, was notorious. It is described in the chronicles of Andrew de Wyntoun and Walter Bower, and their accounts are repeated by later writers such as Hector Boece, John Major and George Buchanan, all of whom present the incident as an example of the barbarous character of the Highlanders. It involved two rival factions named Clan Kay and Clan Quhele, whose identity has always been controversial, but were probably branches or antecedents of the later clans Cameron and Chattan. They had been unable to settle their differences even after the mediation ordered by King Robert III, and so – apparently at the suggestion of the clan chiefs involved – it was agreed that thirty men from each side should fight it out at Perth in a prepared arena in the presence of the king. The arrangement seems to have been little different from many other medieval tournaments, for example the 'Combat of the Thirty' fought between French and English factions in Brittany in 1351, but to commentators like Major, the affair was evidence of the 'savage behaviour' of the 'Wild Scots', whose habit it was to throw aside all caution and rush upon each other 'like bulls'. The stereotype seems justified to some extent on this occasion, because the warriors wore no armour and fought literally to the death, the combat being decided when the last surviving Cameron escaped by swimming the river Tay, leaving just eleven of his opponents still standing. According to Matheson (2014), before the Battle of Dingwall in 1411 between the MacDonalds and the Mackays, the rival leaders agreed to send two champions from each side to duel with each other before the battle commenced. Gilpatrick Roy, the Abbot of Applecross in Wester Ross, was one of those who fought for the MacDonalds, and he was killed by his opponent, but this does not seem to have influenced the outcome of the battle, since the MacDonalds were subsequently victorious.

Nevertheless, this sort of regulated and limited encounter was by no means the norm, and we shall see several examples of clan leaders employing quite sophisticated tactics on the battlefield. Most campaigns were also accompanied not just by merciless fighting but by looting, burning and killing directed against the civilian population. Blood feuds were common. Campbell (1862) rather implausibly denies this on the grounds that there is no word in Gaelic corresponding to 'revenge', but he was an unashamed apologist for the old clans in an age when the English and the Lowland Scots still regarded them as barbarians. Anyone still inclined to subscribe to his idea of Highland warfare as romantic and chivalrous should remember the instances discussed below in which churches were burnt with all their occupants – sometimes fighting men, but just as often women, children and priests who had sought the sanctuary of consecrated ground. Or consider J. Mackay's account of the 'boy killing raid' (Mackay, 1924), which he relates almost incidentally as background to another tale of archery: sometime in the sixteenth century, when the MacDonalds of the Trotternish Peninsula on the north coast of Skye were away on a raid, their neighbours the MacLeods decided that the best legacy they could leave their successors would be to invade Trotternish and slaughter all the boy children, thus weakening their enemies for the future. Twelve MacLeods made their way onto the peninsula, which they supposed was occupied only by women, children and old men, breaking into the houses one by one and murdering every boy they found. On this occasion, however, one fighting man had been left behind – William MacArthur of Kilvaxter, near the northern tip of Trotternish, who although famed for his skill as an archer had not been able to take the field with the others, apparently on account of his dwarfism. William's wife heard the news of the attack and hid their son, still in his cradle, in a pile of peats before rushing into the fields to warn her husband. William returned home and collected his bow and twelve arrows, then took up the trail of the MacLeods, who finding no victims among the alerted population of Kilvaxter had begun to retrace their steps. William, it is said, stalked them all the way to the Snizort

River, which marked the boundary of the MacDonald lands, picking them off until only one man and one arrow remained. He allowed the survivor to escape, not wishing to leave himself without any arrows in case of trouble on the way home. But this version of a happy ending should not distract us from the underlying reality: that one group of supposedly Christian Scots was prepared to commit what would today be regarded as genocide against their neighbours, regardless of the cultural and family ties that linked them.

Another recurring theme in accounts of clan warfare is the extremely high casualty rate on the battlefield, which writers often attribute to the savagery of the 'Wild Scots' and their refusal to give or ask for quarter. We are often told that in battles like Druim na Coub and Blar na Leine the victors as well as the vanquished were almost wiped out. As we shall see, these claims are highly unlikely to be accurate, but it is easy to imagine that a combination of effective close combat weaponry, outdated armour and a cultural emphasis on personal heroics in combat could lead to unusually heavy losses. Unfortunately, we have no direct evidence to show whether or not this was actually the case. Elsewhere in Europe – for example at Visby in Sweden and Towton in Yorkshire – archaeologists have occasionally found mass graves related to particular battles, which have enabled them to draw conclusions about the nature and intensity of the fighting, but none of the Highland battlefields has yet yielded anything of this nature. Neil Grant (2020) notes a difference between the wounds on the skeletons at Visby (1361) and those from Towton a hundred years later. In the former case, many of the injuries were to the legs, while at Towton, head wounds were predominant. This might be attributable to the change from single-handed swords and shields to heavy two-handed weapons such as axes and bills, though there are other possible explanations; the Towton victims, for instance, are sometimes thought to have been executed after the battle rather than killed during the fighting.

What we do have are roughly contemporary descriptions of the aftermath of sixteenth- and seventeenth-century Scottish battles, like that of William Patten at Pinkie in 1547: 'Some with their legs cut off; some but ham-strung, and left lying half dead: others with the arms cut off; divers their necks half asunder; many their heads cloven: of sundry the brains smashed out; some others again, their heads quite off…' (quoted in Carlton, 2011). Drummond (1842) relates the horror of English officers examining their dead after a fight with the Camerons in 1654: 'The deep wownds and terrible slashes that appeared on these mangled carcasses seemed to be above the strength of man… There were some that had their bellys laid open, and others with their arms, thighs, and leggs, lopt off in an amazing manner.' Nevertheless, the Highlanders 'appeared to be no extraordinarey men neither in size or strength'. The explanation, says Drummond, is that when a Highlander strikes with a sword, 'he draws it with great address the whole length of the blade, whereas an unskilfull person takes in no more of it than the breadth of the place where he hitts'. In other words, the clansman did not simply chop with his sword, but used a drawing or slicing cut such as was practised with the Japanese katana, bringing more of the cutting edge into contact with the wound to widen and deepen it. This technique is usually associated with sabres and similarly curved blades, but evidently, the Highlanders were able to achieve similar results with their straight-edged weapons, possibly including axes as well as swords. For this, it was necessary for the blade to be extremely sharp, or, as Drummond puts it, 'of excellent temper'. It must also have been advisable for the swordsmen to practise their skills regularly. We have little information on precisely how this was done, but Loades (2010) quotes a fifteenth-century English manuscript that describes knights striking at a wooden post or pell with wooden swords of twice the normal weight in order to build up their muscles, while also carrying a double weight shield. Highlanders of the '*daoine uasile*' class, who lived off the rents received from their tenants and so were not obliged to spend their days farming or herding cattle, probably did train regularly using similar methods.

Traditional accounts of clan warfare often mention large numbers of heads being severed. Mackenzie (1898) tells how during the battle of

Knockfarrel in 1502, Hector Roy Mackenzie and his men ambushed a party of Munros in a defile, and with their axes and two-edged swords 'cut off so many heads in that small space that, tumbling down the slope to the well, nineteen heads were counted in it'. Bishop Leslie of Ross describes Highland swords as being sharp enough to cut a man in half with a single blow. However, it is likely that most of the heads featured in the stories were cut off after death as trophies rather than in actual combat. Severed heads, especially in wells, are a recurring theme that probably harks back to very ancient ritual practices. The best known of many examples is the famous Well of the Seven Heads on the shore of Loch Oich, which commemorates the place where the heads of seven victims of the Keppoch Murders of 1663 were washed after their deaths. They were killed in revenge for the murder of Alasdair MacDonell of Keppoch, and the grisly trophies were later presented to his kinsman, MacDonell of Glengarry.

Castles

John Major noted that the Scots had never favoured walled towns for defence; he says that Perth was the only example in the country, although in fact Edinburgh had been fortified in the 1450s. Lindesay of Pitscottie adds that they trusted in their physical strength rather than in walls to defend themselves. There were in any case no towns of any size in the Highlands, but castles or smaller fortified houses were very common. Major says that there were as many as two of these to every league, but most were not very strong and not protected by entrenchments outside the walls, in part because the occupants were afraid that they might be occupied by an enemy and held against them. This fear was well founded, because English armies had frequently made use of local fortifications during the Wars of Independence, and might explain why Highland strongholds tended to change hands fairly easily. But in the West Highlands and the Islands, castles, in conjunction with sea power, were a vital part of the military system. Beginning with the first stone defensive works in twelfth-century

Orkney and Caithness, they had spread rapidly across the country until, by the fifteenth century, every clan of consequence had its own stronghold. In the west, most were located on or close to the seashore, where they could protect not just the chiefs and their retinues but the fleets of galleys that were vital to their military and economic power. They were so thickly planted that in many places – for example the Sound of Mull, which separates that island from the mainland – a ship sailing along the coast in reasonable visibility would always be within sight of at least one of them. Among the best known are Dunstaffnage near Oban, opposite the south-eastern end of the sound, which by the fifteenth century was held by the Campbells, and the MacLean stronghold of Duart across the water, on the coast of Mull itself. The Ardnamurchan Peninsula was the site of Mingary castle, on the northern side of the Sound of Mull, which will feature prominently in our story, and Castle Tioram, which belonged to the MacDonalds of Clanranald, on the other side of the peninsula. Further north on the west coast are Dunvegan on Skye, the seat of the MacLeods of Harris, and the Mackenzie stronghold of Eilean Donan on the nearby mainland, strategically located at the confluence of three sea lochs. On the north coast, Castle Varrich, the headquarters of the Mackays, differs from those in the west by being built not on the seashore but on a prominent hill high above the inlet known as the Kyle of Tongue, while in eastern Sutherland, Dunrobin, home of the earls of Sutherland, is almost a quarter of a mile from the sea – proof if it were needed that the Mackays and Sutherlands were not sea powers. Inland, along the important strategic route of the Great Glen, castles at Dingwall, Inverness, Urquhart on Loch Ness and Inverlochy near present-day Fort William guarded the lines of communication from Argyll north-eastwards to the Moray Firth, and the kings of Scots always tried to ensure that they remained in the hands of the monarchy or local magnates of certain loyalty. Conversely, the clans of the west coast and the isles regularly attacked them, often successfully.

In a few places where up-to-date fortifications were lacking, the remains of very ancient structures, which can still be found scattered across the northern and western Highlands, could still play a defensive role. Vitrified forts like Dun Lagaidh on Loch Broom in Wester Ross were built in the early Iron Age around 700 BC, constructed of stone on a frame of timber, which was then apparently fired deliberately. The reason for this is still unclear, though it may have been thought that the heat would fuse the stones together and provide extra strength. Although long abandoned by our period, the walls were often still solid enough to give useful protection, and Dun Lagaidh seems to have been intermittently occupied as late as 1230 and possibly even later (Matheson, 2014). The tall, open-roofed and windowless stone towers known as brochs date from the Roman era or soon after, but we hear of them still being used for defensive purposes in the Viking era. The example at Dun Carloway in Lewis, part of which still survives, was in good enough condition in the sixteenth century that it could be used as a refuge by cattle raiders. A local tradition records that these men were cornered by their pursuers, but fought off all attempts to capture them until a certain Donald Cam MacAulay climbed the external wall by means of knives stuck between the stones and threw burning heather inside, forcing them to surrender. The shape of a broch closely resembles a chimney, which probably gives a good indication of the effect of fire on its defenders, but clearly it might be considered a feasible option if hard-pressed by a more powerful enemy.

Ships

Ever since the days of the Vikings, wooden ships, propelled by both sails and oars, had been a fundamental part of life on the West Highland mainland as well as in the Isles, replacing the hide-covered boats that had been in use previously. The large number of inhabited islands in the Hebrides and the indented nature of the mainland coast, with its long sea lochs leading as much as 30 miles into the interior, made seagoing vessels essential for trade and everyday communication as well as warfare. The ships of the later Middle Ages differed only in minor details from the Viking longships, and are generally referred to in English as galleys. The Gaelic terms are usually Anglicised as '*lymphads*' and '*birlinns*', the former being derived from '*long fada*', which literally means 'longship'. The precise distinction between the two types is unclear, if in fact there was one, but *lymphads* seem generally to have been larger, with between twenty and forty rowers, while *birlinns* could have as few as sixteen. (See also the discussion in Chapter 1 of *The Highland Battles.*) There were also '*nyvaigs*', often translated as 'little ships', which might have included the eight-oared boats mentioned in a Privy Council minute of 1615 (Rixson). The same document states that the carrying capacity of these vessels was estimated at three fighting men per oar.

Wallace Clark (1993) sailed a small replica galley of sixteen oars, the *Aileach*, from Ireland to Lewis in 1991, and provides some interesting information on the performance of these vessels, although it is reasonable to suppose that the experienced seamen of the late Middle Ages would have managed to get slightly more out of them in an emergency. Speeds of up to 12 knots were recorded under sail with a following wind, but over a two-day period, the average speed was 2.8 knots. This nevertheless equates to about 75 miles per day, which was much more than could have been achieved travelling by land. Clark did not feel that changing direction across the wind by tacking was practical in any sort of swell, and in *Aileach*, this manoeuvre was always done by wearing, or turning the bows away from the wind. This was safer but more time-consuming than tacking, and in a force 4 breeze, the vessel drifted downwind three boat lengths every time it was attempted. Under oars it was possible to make 4 knots for a brief period, but sustained speed was about half of this, especially if there was a headwind or heavy sea. Rowing was found to be ineffective in waves more than 4 feet high, which means anything above force 4, a 13-knot 'moderate breeze', on the Beaufort wind scale used for marine forecasts today. To put this into perspective, the annual average wind speed is about 12 knots at Stornoway on the relatively sheltered east coast of the Isle of Lewis, and 14 knots on the exposed Inner Hebridean island of Tiree (metoffice.gov.uk). The obvious conclusion to be drawn from this is that manoeuvre under oars was feasible only in good weather or in sheltered waters, while even under sail, moderate winds were preferable if any changes of heading were contemplated. However, it should be borne in mind that in the heyday of the galleys the rowing was done by picked crews with a great deal of experience in the job and a strong sense of pride and professionalism in doing it, and they might well have been able to manage somewhat rougher waters. The seas surrounding the Hebrides are particularly challenging to navigate because of the unpredictable weather and the complex topography, with the narrow straits between islands often funnelling the seas into dangerous currents. Details of how ships were navigated in the Middle Ages are scarce, but Rixson points out that knowing one's position was seldom a problem, at least in good visibility, as there are few places in the Isles where a ship is not in view of the mainland or a number of islands. Martin Martin says that the islanders of Saint Kilda would forecast the weather by watching the sky, which is a fairly reliable method as the prevailing winds are from the west, and approaching cloud formations can be seen while still far out to sea. They could tell direction when out of sight of land from the sun, moon and stars or by following flocks of migrating sea birds; the behaviour of birds could also give warning of storms.

Nevertheless, unexpected bad weather was always a risk, and one of the most famous Gaelic poems of all time concerns a ship that survived a terrifying storm. The 'Birlinn Claoine Raghnaill' or 'Clanranald's Birlinn', written by the eighteenth-century bard Alasdair mac Mhaighstir Alasdair, describes a sea voyage by the chief of Clan Ranald from the Hebrides to Ireland. Denis Rixson points out that by the time Alasdair wrote, the age of the galley was almost over, and the Clanranalds must have been among the very last to possess a seaworthy *birlinn*. Some aspects of the poem are anachronistic for the eighteenth century, for example, the mention of 'heavy coats of mail' and 'bows of yew', but this makes it more likely that it preserves a genuine memory of an earlier period when the galleys were the capital ships of the island clans. The ship itself is described as black, being protected against the elements by a coat of pitch, and the oars as white and made of pine wood. An alert and serious man would be selected as the helmsman, another would be placed in charge of the equipment, and a further five of various aspects of the sails. There was also a bailer, who needed steady nerves, as he would only be called upon if the ship were in danger of flooding. A lookout was appointed to watch for landmarks on the shore and correct the steering if necessary, while the captain was accompanied by another crewman whose job it was to keep an eye on the state of the sea and report any signs of danger. A nervous and prudent character was best for this job, as it was vital that the alarm be given quickly and in a loud voice if squalls or heavy seas threatened the vessel. No one else was to report on anything happening on the water, because too much shouting would lead only to confusion. The perils of a storm at sea are vividly described in the poem, but its reassuring message is that if faced with courage, and with the help of God and the Holy Spirit, the sea will eventually become humble and quiet, just as an adversary on land will give way if you remain undaunted. No doubt spiritual comfort was always considered essential for men risking their lives on the ocean, and Rixson quotes several traditional prayers that were offered on setting out or at the hoisting of the sails. Among the numerous Hebridean superstitions listed by Martin Martin was the idea that a boat should be rowed in a circle 'sunwise', or, in other words, clockwise, on setting out in order to bring luck.

The ship would normally be rowed out of its sheltered harbour to a point in open water where the sails would be hoisted, though it might be rowed for extended periods in calm weather or when advancing to battle. When under oars one of the men would lead the others in a rowing song or '*iorram*', of which an example – probably more expertly composed than the average – is included in the poem. It describes the glowing cheeks, sweat dripping from faces and blistered and peeling palms that must have been the usual lot of the galley crews. And yet after perhaps several hours of this hard labour, they might have been called upon to take up their weapons and fight for their lives in the crush of a boarding fight, with no way of escape if they were defeated except into the sea. Highland galleys were generally small and light enough to be drawn up on a beach or even dragged overland for short distances. In at least some cases, the planks that made up their hulls were fixed together by wooden pins, so that the whole vessel could be taken to pieces by withdrawing the pins, and almost as quickly reassembled. A tradition of the MacLeans relates that Allan MacRuari of Clanranald once escaped from his pursuers after a raid by having his ship disassembled at Salen on the south coast of Ardnamurchan, and the planks carried on the shoulders of the crew to Shielfoot, near Castle Tioram on the north coast of the peninsula, a distance of almost 3 miles (MacLean, 1889).

Chapter 4

Shackling the Calf: The Battle of Druim na Coub

Date: *c.*1433
Location: Near Tongue, Sutherland
Combatants: Clan Mackay versus Sutherlands under Angus Moray
Outcome: Mackay victory

Today, Druim na Coub is one of the most inaccessible spots on the British mainland. It lies in the shadow of the great mountain range of Ben Loyal on the north coast of Scotland, at the head of the small valley that runs into the Atlantic near the tiny village of Tongue, which is itself nearly 40 miles from the nearest settlement of any size. The road that led there had begun two and a half centuries earlier in the country called Moray, on the far side of the Moray Firth. The traditional histories of Clan Mackay claim that their founders were related to the ancient ruling house of Moray, and had been exiled to Sutherland after an unsuccessful rebellion against Scottish rule in the 1160s (MacDougall, 1953.) There is no contemporary evidence for this theory, but it is by no means unlikely. At that time, the Scottish kings were beginning to consolidate their power in the far north, a region that until then had been dominated by the Viking earls of Orkney and Caithness, who had displaced the original Pictish rulers in the ninth century. The establishment of a Scots or Gaelic-speaking colony in Sutherland would obviously have been a logical step in that direction, and it should be noted that throughout their subsequent history the Mackays tended to align themselves with the monarchy in its disputes with other clans, and in particular, the MacDonald

Lords of the Isles, perhaps having learned at a very early date the risks associated with rebellion. According to Angus Mackay in his history of the clan (1906), the name Mackay (Mac Aodh in Gaelic) is related to MacHeth, which was the surname of the rival royal claimants who had caused so much trouble for Malcolm IV and William I in the late twelfth century (see *The Highland Battles*, Chapter 6, for the career of the MacHeths). Recent research (Grannd, 2013) has also suggested that the Mackay dialect of Gaelic has more in common with that of the east coast than with its neighbours in western Sutherland.

Whatever their ultimate origin, the Mackays begin to emerge into history in the early fourteenth century, when they were already in control of two strategically important areas in the far north-west. The first was in the relatively fertile limestone country around Durness, where they had come into possession of former church lands via an alliance with the Bishop of Caithness. Their other stronghold was the broad valley of Strath Naver a few miles further east, which by the 1370s had become a bone of contention between them and the earls of Sutherland. Most of the terrain of what is now the county of Sutherland, apart from the eastern coastal district, is rocky, infertile and swept by strong winds, making it unwelcoming for human settlement. In 1586, William Camden, in his *Britannia*, says of Sutherland that 'By reason of the sharpness of the air it is very thinly inhabited, and thereupon extremely infested with the fiercest of Wolves.' According to a persistent tradition, these animals were so voracious that in some parishes the people found it necessary to bury their dead on offshore islands to prevent them from being dug up and eaten (Ritchie, 1920). However, there are sheltered 'oases' of good soil which, although almost deserted today in the aftermath of the nineteenth-century Clearances, were once more densely populated. Sir Robert Gordon, writing in the early seventeenth century, describes Strath Naver as better for pasture for cattle than arable farming, but says that the river Naver, which runs through it, was rich in salmon, and the sea at its mouth also provided excellent fishing (Gordon, 1813). Apart from Durness and Strath Naver, the largest such region was Assynt on the west coast, which was held in the later Middle Ages by a branch of the MacLeods of Lewis, who were often allied to the Mackays. For the first century or so of their tenure in the north the Mackays seem to have been relatively undisturbed by incursions by neighbouring clans, and grew to become the most numerous of the peoples of the far north-west. But by the fifteenth century, political conditions had changed, and they were now widely regarded as the most warlike. One reason for this was that they needed to be ever more vigilant in defending the right to occupy their lands against encroachment from the south-east, even in times of relatively strong royal authority. This was partly due to the remoteness of their holdings, and partly due to the apparent failure of their chiefs to obtain legal charters to confirm their possession of them even in the fifteenth century, an age when legal title was gradually becoming more important than brute force. As MacDougall (1953) puts it: 'The military ability and fighting qualities of the Mackays have never been doubted, but the same cannot be said of their diplomacy.'

On the east coast of Sutherland, where the land was more fertile and the population more numerous, another clan was continually extending its influence. Their original name was de Moravia, and like the Mackays, they had once lived in Moray, where they traced their ancestry back to Freskin, a Flemish nobleman who had pacified the country in the name of King David I in the early twelfth century. However, unlike the Mackays, they had been on the winning side in the upheavals of that period, and their reward was a grant of land in the richer part of the county, and in the 1230s, a peerage for their leader, William de Moravia, who became the first earl of Sutherland. Angus Mackay (1906) quotes the Blackcastle Manuscript, compiled in 1832 from the papers of the Mackay and Sutherland families, as an important source for the origins of the feud between the two clans. In 1342, the fifth earl, another William de Moravia, received a papal dispensation to marry Margaret Bruce, the daughter of King Robert I and sister of David II. In his application, he referred to an 'ancient enemy' who was said to be guilty of 'murders, burnings, depredations, forays, and other evils'. It is possible, as Angus Mackay and others have supposed, that this enemy was Clan Mackay, but if so we have no evidence regarding the nature of their original dispute, unless the Sutherlands had already laid claim to their neighbours' lands in the north-west. In this connection it is perhaps significant that the eldest sons of the earls seem already to have adopted the courtesy title of Lord Strath Naver, which can hardly be seen as anything other than a statement of overlordship in that district. In 1345, the earl received from his brother-in-law King David II a Grant of Regality confirming the couple and their descendants in possession of extensive lands that did specifically include Strath Naver (MacDougall, 1953). But their only child, John, died in the Black Death and the succession eventually passed to Robert, William's son by his second wife, whose title to Strath Naver was naturally disputed by the de facto chief there, Iye Mackay. In 1370, according to the Blackcastle Manuscript, Iye Mackay and Earl William met at Dingwall to settle the argument in front of a gathering of neutral chiefs. When it became clear that the Mackays were about to win the case, the earl's brother, Nicolas, murdered Iye and his son Donald while they were asleep. Nicolas was forced to flee, pursued by the furious Mackays, and soon afterwards, William himself is known to have died. We have no record of the cause of his death, but it is not unlikely, as Robert Mackay (1829) speculates, that Iye's kinsmen had managed to obtain their revenge. No doubt the feud continued to simmer, but it was not until after Iye's great-grandson, Angus Dubh, succeeded as head of the clan in 1403 that full-scale hostilities began again.

Fortunately, Angus Dubh proved to be equal to the occasion. He has traditionally been regarded as one of the greatest leaders that the Mackays ever had. He was still young when his father died, and under the tutelage of his uncle, Huistean, who had somehow offended his mother, war broke out around 1406 with her people, the MacLeods of Assynt. The latter invaded Strath Naver and retreated southwards with their plunder, but were caught by the Mackays in Strath Oykel and wiped out. The battle became known as *La Tuiteam Tarbhach*, or 'The Day of Great Slaughter', and Sir Robert Gordon claimed that only one MacLeod escaped alive. Equally implausibly, in view of the relations between the two clans, he alleged that victory was assured by the presence of a contingent sent by Earl Robert of Sutherland to help the Mackays. The latter, naturally, have always argued that this was simply an attempt to take the credit for their feat of arms and to establish the Sutherlands as the feudal overlords of the Mackays, and that the Sutherlands were in fact quite happy to see them occupied elsewhere. In 1411, when Donald of the Isles launched his invasion of Ross, Angus Dubh brought his clan out against him. At this time, Angus was said to have had 4,000 men under his command; this was a very powerful force by clan standards, but presumably includes a large contingent of allied clans, because two decades later, the Mackays were only able to muster 1,200 for the decisive fight at Druim na Coub. According to Sir Robert Gordon, Angus only agreed to join the war because Donald had injured some Mackay allies in the districts that he had invaded, but it was the beginning of a long tradition of the clan taking the side of the monarchy against the rebellious western clans. A battle was fought in the vicinity of Dingwall between the Mackays and their allies on the one side, and perhaps 10,000 men under Donald (though the latter's army may have been somewhat smaller than this – see page 16 for John Sadler's estimate for the Battle of Harlaw). We have no details of the course of this fight, but the outnumbered Mackays were eventually dispersed, Angus's brother was killed and he himself was captured. He was imprisoned for a while on the west coast, but after his defeat at Harlaw Donald found himself in desperate need of allies, so he released Angus and arranged a marriage between him and Donald's own sister. To cement the new alliance Donald granted Strath Halladale, on the border between Sutherland and Caithness, to the Mackays. This of course cost Donald nothing since he had never controlled the district, and is a classic example of the trouble that these reckless grants could cause. In 1415, Angus took an army to occupy the valley, though it seems that he met with opposition because, according to Hector Boece, he raided into Caithness and Moray, in both of which the heirs of his family's enemy Nicolas of Sutherland held extensive lands, and returned with a great deal of loot. At this point, King James I was still a prisoner in England and royal authority in the far north was non-existent, so it is highly likely, as Angus Mackay (1906) suggests, that his namesake took advantage of that fact to seek revenge against the Sutherlands. In 1426, he again invaded Caithness and won a hard-fought battle against an unidentified enemy at Harpsdale, 2 miles outside the village of Halkirk. But by this time, King James had been released from his captivity and returned to Scotland determined to restore order by any means necessary. In 1427, he summoned the unsuspecting northern chiefs to a parliament at Inverness and arrested them en masse. Some were executed for various specific crimes, but others, including Angus Dubh, were released in exchange for hostages. Thus Angus returned to Strath Naver while his eldest son, Neil, spent the next few years in prison on the inaccessible Bass Rock, from which he took his nickname of Neil Vass, or 'of the Bass'. Meanwhile, Angus's cousin, Thomas Neilson Mackay of Creich, who held much of Strath Halladale from Angus, had continued to pursue the feud with the leading families of Caithness and Moray. In the course of these activities, he had set fire to the chapel of St Duthus at Tain, trapping one of his enemies, Mowat of Freswick, inside and killing him. The king immediately outlawed Thomas and declared his lands in Creich and Strath Halladale forfeit, giving away much of the latter to a certain Angus Moray, a leading retainer of the Sutherlands.

Angus Moray forthwith began to plan an expedition to the Mackay country. The ostensible aim was to take possession of Strath Halladale in accordance with King James's decree, but in the view of Angus Mackay, the real aim of the invaders was the complete destruction of Angus Dubh and the seizure of all his clan's lands. This would explain why, instead of invading Strath Halladale, Angus Moray advanced directly on the Mackay chief's stronghold at Castle Varrich on the Kyle of Tongue, on the north coast west of Strath Naver. Various dates are given in different accounts, but it is most likely that the invasion took place between 1431 and 1433. The expedition travelled via Lairg and Loch Shin, with around 1,500 men recruited in Sutherland, possibly including a contingent supplied by the earl of Sutherland himself, and commanded by Angus Moray and his two sons-in-law, Morgan and Neil. Angus Dubh was apparently reluctant to advance south to meet them because of the threat of being taken in the flank by the clans of Caithness, who might have been tempted to take advantage of the situation to avenge their defeat at Harpsdale. The clan historians all argue that it must have also been a deliberate strategy to lure the enemy as far north as possible before bringing them to battle – a plan that would both give the Mackays time to mobilise their forces and ensure that the invaders would find it impossible to escape if they were defeated. The Mackays had only about 1,200 men, and were forced to take the field without their most experienced commanders: Angus's cousin Thomas had eventually been captured and executed for his attack on the chapel at Tain, while the chief's son Neil was still a hostage on the Bass Rock. Angus himself was now of advanced years and so infirm that he had to be carried on a litter. Field command therefore devolved upon Angus's son by his second wife, Iain Aberach, 'the man of Lochaber', so called because he had recently returned from that district, where he had been fostered by his mother's MacDonald relatives. A rather unlikely story would have it that his father tested him on his return home by making him fight a savage boarhound for his dinner – a test that he passed with flying colours. Iain had already earned a reputation as a swordsman, but is said to have been still in his teens, too young to have gained any experience of commanding troops, and when the news of his appointment somehow reached the Sutherland men they greeted it with derision, threatening to put a cow shackle on the 'calf', as they called him.

But Iain soon proved to be a talented war leader, perhaps having learned something of the art during his stay with the MacDonalds. The place where he chose to meet the invaders was at Druim na Coub on the slopes of the Ben Loyal range, no more than 3 miles from Castle Varrich. The long ridge known as Ben Loyal consists of four rocky granite peaks, which extend for about 3 miles north to south inland of Tongue, and rise to a height of approximately 2,500 feet. The ridge itself would have been virtually impassable to an army, which left Angus Moray with two possible approach routes, either north or south of the mountain. The position in which Iain Aberach chose to meet him was north-west of the high ground, and between it and the inlet of the sea known as the Kyle of Tongue. The place name Druim na Coub does not appear on modern maps and its meaning in Gaelic is obscure, but Gunn and Mackay (1897) render it as 'Druim-na-cupa', which would signify 'the ridge of the cup'. The most likely location is the ridge that is marked on the modern OS Landranger map as Carn Fada, or 'the long hill', and it is tempting to link the older name to the prehistoric cup and ring marks that can still be seen on stones near the northern end of the feature. If this is the correct location, the Mackays would have been drawn up in a very strong position near the summit of Carn Fada, with the marshy valley of the stream known today as the Rhian Burn to their front and an unbroken line of sight to the east and south. The small body of water known as Loch Hakon (Lochan Hakel on the modern OS map) and the marshy ground surrounding it at the northern end of the ridge would have provided additional protection against being outflanked from that direction. If the enemy marched around the eastern and northern slopes of Ben Loyal and then turned right towards Tongue, they would expose their left flank to a downhill charge from the higher ground, while if they advanced from the south via the narrow 'Bealach Dubh', or Black Pass, between Ben Loyal and Loch an Dithreibh, they would have to do so in a column with a frontage of only two or three men. Their approach would also be visible to the defenders from a distance of at least a mile as soon as they began to descend. In either case, they would be tired by the long march, while the waiting defenders were still fresh as well as having the advantage of the higher ground. As an additional precaution, a detachment of Mackays was hidden in a copse 'on the side of the pass' (Gunn & Mackay), from where they could ambush the rear of the enemy column as it passed by. There does not appear to be a suitable copse in the right area now, though there are patches of woodland further down the Rhian Burn towards Tongue.

According to Gunn and Mackay, scouts posted at the southern end of Ben Loyal reported that the Sutherland men were, as expected, taking the most direct way to Tongue via that route, following a track that passed close to the foot of Carn Fada. Soon they came into sight over the Black Pass, advancing in a 'disorderly manner' rather than deploying into line of battle, as if they expected to meet no serious opposition. Perhaps they were encouraged by the apparent small size of the part of the defending army that they could see, as well as by the supposed inexperience of its commander. But Iain Aberach was managing his men with impressive skill. Sir Robert Gordon says that Angus Dubh sent a message offering Neil and Morgan all of his lands except part of Strath Naver in return for peace, but that this was refused. In contrast, Robert Mackay (1829) states that 'there was no parley', but the battle was joined at once. As the Sutherland men approached them, the Mackays showered them with arrows from long range, provoking them into an impetuous charge. Robert Mackay says that the defenders charged down to meet them, preventing them from deploying their full strength, so that many of the Sutherland men were still trying to get forward when battle was joined. For a while, the hand-to-hand fighting on the hill was fierce, but the Mackays stood firm long enough for the hidden detachment to emerge from the wood and rout the rearmost invaders, who were still advancing along the track to join the fight. Then they swung westwards and fell on the left flank of the Sutherland main body just as it was starting to fall back. The result was that Angus Moray's force suddenly disintegrated, and the survivors turned and fled up the northern slopes of Ben Loyal. Angus and both his sons-in-law, who had been well to the front, were killed on the field along with about half of their men (Robert Mackay), and the remainder of the fugitives were harried as far as a ford called Ath Charrie, 8 miles away, which Angus Mackay describes as being on a stream running into Loch Loyal. There a stone once marked the grave of the last of the Sutherland men to be overtaken.

It is probably this encounter that John Major is referring to when he describes 'a fierce battle between Angus Duff and Angus Moray at Strathnaver', though he dates it to 1431, the same year as Donald Balloch's victory at Inverlochy. Sutherland losses were clearly very heavy, but despite Bower's and Major's assertions it seems improbable that the Mackays had suffered to a comparable extent. Iain Aberach was said by Robert Gordon to have lost an arm in the fight, and the account in 'Conflicts of the Clans' goes further, alleging that he 'lost all his men' and was himself left for dead on the field and only rescued after the battle. But as he was to lead his clan in battle for many years to come, and maintain his reputation for 'great strength of body' in Robert Mackay's words, as well as courage, fortitude, and 'all the social virtues', it is unlikely that Iain was actually seriously disabled in the action. There was, however, one great tragedy for the Mackays still to result from the battle. Robert Mackay goes on to tell us that a certain Iver of Shiness on Loch Shin, a member of the Matheson clan who is described as a follower of the earl of Sutherland, and presumably owed him military service for his lands in that county, had refused to join Angus Moray's army when it passed through the village. But on the day that it set out, his wife served him porridge for breakfast, which was evidently not his usual fare. When he asked the reason for this, he was bluntly told that porridge was the proper food for cowards, at which he put on his armour and stormed out after the departing army, warning his wife that if he went, neither of them would ever again enjoy peace. By the time Iver caught up with Moray's men at Druim na Coub the battle was over, the Sutherland men were in full flight and the Mackays were running in pursuit. The field was almost deserted, but old Angus Dubh Mackay, who had watched the battle from a nearby hill, had now arrived to inspect the site and was wandering about trying to identify the casualties, supported by a servant. Iver took cover behind a bush, and then in a moment of madness he drew his bow and launched an arrow at the chief before taking to his heels. Angus was fatally wounded, the last and most unnecessary casualty of the battle, and although Iver succeeded in escaping to his home, he was to be, as he had predicted, a fugitive for the rest of his life.

Sir Robert Gordon alleges that Iain Aberach was forced to flee to the Hebrides after the battle for fear of reprisals by the Sutherlands, and that eventually he went to Dunrobin as a supplicant and received a pardon. Angus Mackay (1906) understandably dismisses this story as propaganda, arguing that 'unless the Earl of Sutherland was able to raise the dead on the slopes of Ben Loyal by the blast of a trumpet' he no longer had an army capable of resuming the offensive. However, Mackay does admit that for a while Iain was in fear of assassins sent by the relatives of some of the men he had killed, so that he often slept in a hideout in the hills near Castle Varrich, which became known as Leabaidh Ian Aberich, or Iain Aberach's bed. In fact, as Mackay points out, it was probably only a threat from a different quarter that prevented the victorious Mackays from taking the offensive into Sutherland. Not long after the battle at Druim na Coub another engagement was fought at Tom an Dris, on the river Halladale on the border between the Mackay country and Caithness. Few details survive, but it seems that Iain Aberach drew up his army on the west side of the river to resist an invasion by the men of Caithness. Robert Mackay points out that his tactics were very similar to those employed at Druim na Coub; first standing on the defensive in a strong position with his back to a hill, then counterattacking once the enemy was sufficiently weakened. A large number of human bones found in the area in the 1820s testified to the slaughter of the Caithness men as they tried to retreat across the river (Mackay, 1829).

Then, in 1437, King James I, whose popularity had waned following his brutal attempts to curb the power of his own nobles, was assassinated by agents in the pay of the earl of Atholl. In the ensuing confusion, Neil Vass escaped from his prison on the Bass Rock with the help of the governor's wife, who was related to the Mackays, and returned home to take over command of the clan. In the following year, he decided on an invasion of Caithness. Angus Mackay says that some of the clansmen wanted to keep Iain Aberach as chief, but the latter refused to compete against his older brother. Neil rewarded him by granting him lands in Strath Naver, but according to Mackay custom, no written charter was given or asked for, which in later years would leave the grant open to a legal challenge by the Sutherlands. Neil was nevertheless aware that he was inexperienced in warfare thanks to his long imprisonment, and so he placed Iain in command of the Caithness expedition, which marched east by the northern coastal route and advanced on Thurso. The Caithness men met them outside the town and the invaders retreated with their spoils until they reached Sandside Bay, which is situated on the coast east of the mouth of the river Halladale, about 15 miles west of Thurso. There the Mackay main body turned to fight, but as the Caithness men drew up for battle, a reserve corps of Mackays, which Iain had posted on a nearby ridge known as Druim Hollistan, emerged and attacked their flank. Iain Aberach's men quickly trapped the enemy against the sea, killed many, and chased the survivors back towards Thurso. The vigorous pursuit by the Mackays gave the encounter the name of *Ruaig Handside*, or the Sandside Chase. None of the early sources for this or the previous battle specify who the Caithness men were, but there is reason to believe that these events mark the beginning of a feud between the Mackays and the Gunns, which would have consequences in a much later campaign (see the Battle of Torran Dubh, Chapter 9), if in fact the Gunns had not already come to blows with the Mackays at Harpsdale a decade earlier. Clan Gunn was an ancient family that held land in Caithness and eastern Sutherland, and claimed descent from the Norse earls of Orkney; their eponymous founder was Gunni, a grandson of the famous Orkney pirate Sven Asleifsson. They seem to have been especially noted as skilled archers. Robert Mackay relates a story of the Sandside battle, which he says was still told 'of a winter's night'. A powerful Strath Naver man named Alastair Balloch had been wielding a great axe and carrying all before him in the fight, but as the enemy fell back and he began to pursue them he encountered a small, agile Gunn warrior who was covering the retreat. Avoiding Alastair's blows, the Gunn managed to get behind him and hamstring him with his sword, bringing him helpless to the ground. Alastair was carried off the field cursing the man who had outwitted him, and when he recovered, he returned to Caithness in an unsuccessful search for revenge. It was said that when he eventually died, overcome by depression at his perceived humiliation, he refused the priest's injunction to forgive all his enemies, and announced that if he was to go to hell on that account he looked forward to catching up with the little Gunn there!

Iver of Shiness was eventually hunted down and assassinated by the Mackays, but according to the custom of the time, the death of the chief could only be expiated by the revenge killing of a man of equal rank, in this case the chief of the Mathesons, Alister MacMurchy, whose headquarters were in Lochalsh, on the west coast opposite the Isle of Skye. The Mackays seem not to have possessed a fleet and had no easy land route to Lochalsh, so for a few years vengeance was postponed, but in 1437, the assassination of King James I temporarily removed the threat of royal intervention and provided the Mackays with their opportunity. As a leading member of the regency that followed during the minority of James II, Alexander MacDonald, Lord of the Isles, was appointed Justiciar of the North and came into possession of the earldom of Ross, which his family had long coveted. Alexander was related to the Mackays by marriage and also had a longstanding dispute with the Mathesons, so he was happy to allow a Mackay army to march through Ross. On learning of their approach, Alister MacMurchy and his four sons marched eastwards to meet them, but were ambushed at Poul an Tarie in Glen Udalain, about 6 miles east of where Kyle of Lochalsh now stands. The Matheson army was completely destroyed, and its chief and all four of his sons were killed. It took nearly a century for Clan Matheson to regain its power (Matheson, 2014). Angus Dubh had finally been avenged, but the threat from the Sutherlands would re-emerge long before the century was out.

Tongue today is a small settlement on the Kyle of Tongue on the north coast of Sutherland. It is not easily accessible by public transport, though currently there is a minibus service from Lairg every Wednesday (see transportfortongue.co.uk for details). Tongue

Mail armour and two-handed sword from Dunvegan Castle, from G.B.N. Hill, *Footsteps of Dr Johnson*, London 1890. Probably sixteenth century; traditionally attributed to Sir Ruairidh Mor MacLeod (died 1626). (*Author*)

The carved grave slabs in West Highland churchyards are among the best evidence available for the appearance of the warriors of the time. These are in the Poltalloch Enclosure at St Columba's Church, Kilmartin, Argyllshire, and are believed to date from the fourteenth or fifteenth centuries. Note the open-faced bascinet helmets with mail coifs, long mail coats and single-handed swords. (*Visit Scotland/Paul Tomkins*)

It is often argued that the nobility of the Highland clans would have adopted the styles of armour and dress popular among their contemporaries in the rest of Europe. This reconstruction by the re-enactment group Medieval Realm of Aberdeen shows how such warriors may have appeared in the early to mid-fifteenth century. (*Harry Brechin*)

Dunvegan Castle, Skye, the headquarters of the MacLeods of Harris and home of the Fairy Flag. (*Visit Scotland/Kenny Lam*)

Looking west towards the Kyle of Tongue from Brae Tongue. In the middle distance, at the north end of the ridge known as An Garbh-chnoc, are the ruins of Castle Varrich, once the stronghold of the Mackays. (*Author*)

The Bass Rock in the Firth of Forth, where Neil 'Vass' Mackay was imprisoned during the Druim na Coub campaign. Tantallon Castle is in the foreground. (*Visit Scotland/Kenny Lam*)

The Ben Loyal range seen from the south, on the route of Angus Moray's march from Lairg. The two viable routes to Tongue pass on either side of this formidable obstacle. (*Author*)

A view southwards from Brae Tongue, looking towards the Druim na Coub battlefield along the valley of the Rhian Burn, with Ben Loyal on the left and the Bealach Dubh or Black Pass on the horizon in the centre. (*Author*)

The low ridge in the middle distance of this picture is Carn Fada, with the waters of Loch Hakon visible in front. It was probably on this ridge that Iain Aberach drew up his men to await the Sutherland army, and down its slopes in the direction of the camera that the defeated Sutherland men retreated. (*Author*)

The northern end of the Ben Loyal range. The Sutherland survivors fled eastwards around the mountain towards the left of the picture, pursued by the Mackays. (*Author*)

The view northwards from Ardnamurchan Point, the most westerly point of the British mainland, towards the isles of Rum and Skye. Traditionally, the Ardnamurchan Peninsula marked the boundary between the Southern and Northern Hebrides. It was through this strait that Angus Og's galleys passed on their way to Bloody Bay. (*Author*)

Duart Castle on Mull, the stronghold of the MacLeans of Duart, who led the forces loyal to Lord John of the Isles at Bloody Bay. (*Visit Scotland/Kenny Lam*)

Looking south from the hills above Kilchoan on the Ardnamurchan Peninsula, across Loch Sunart to the north coast of Mull. Bloody Bay is on the opposite side of the loch. (*Author*)

The beach at Bloody Bay, looking west from near Tobermory lighthouse. (*Author*)

Strath Oykel, Sutherland, looking north-westwards from near Carbisdale Castle in the direction of the Mackay country. The site of the Battle of Aldicharrish has not been identified, but is thought to have been somewhere in the lower reaches of this valley, which was a major east–west route in the Middle Ages. (*Author*)

The Church of Saint Maelrubha at Contin, Easter Ross, built on the site of the chapel burnt by the MacDonalds during their advance to Blar na Parc. (*Author*)

Loch Kinellan from the south-west. The crannog or artificial island where the Mackenzies may have had their headquarters is now overgrown with bushes but is just visible in the centre, close to the shore. One theory places the site of the Battle of Blar na Parc in the fields just to the right of the loch, although no archaeological finds have been made to confirm this. (*Author*)

Another possible site for the Blar na Parc battlefield is in the woods a few hundred yards west of the viewpoint in the previous photograph. This fits slightly better with accounts describing two low rises facing each other across an expanse of bog, with the Mackenzies holding the high ground on the far right of the picture and the MacDonalds advancing from left to right. As can be seen, the ground here is still very marshy. (*Author*)

A view of the battlefield of Flodden, Northumberland, from the position of the West Highland contingents on the Scottish right. While James IV met his death at the hands of the English billmen in a bog at the bottom of the slope, the Highlanders were taken unawares in the flank and routed with heavy losses. (*Megan Peers*)

Where the Rough Bounds meet the Great Glen: Ben Tee seen from Laggan Locks. It was on the slopes of this mountain that the Frasers first saw the Clanranald army descending towards the battlefield at Blar na Leine with its banners displayed. (*Visit Scotland/Luigi di Pasquale*)

A view south-westwards towards Loch Lochy from the point where the modern Caledonian Canal enters the loch at Laggan Locks. The Clanranalds and their allies marched along the slopes of the hills in the distance to intercept the Frasers near this spot. (*Author*)

Looking north-east towards the head of Loch Lochy. The battle of Blar na Leine is usually assumed to have been fought on the flat ground in the middle distance, but the water level has risen since the 1540s and much of the site is now submerged. (*Author*)

The ruins of Urquhart Castle near Drumnadrochit, seen from Loch Ness. In the sixteenth century, the castle was a stronghold of the Grants, allies of the Frasers. It was sacked by the MacDonalds on at least three occasions in the first half of the century, on the last occasion by the victorious Iain Moidertach in 1545, after the Battle of Blar na Leine. (*Kate Peers*)

can be reached by car via the A836, travelling either east from Thurso (42 miles) or north from Lairg (37 miles). The first 30 miles or so of the drive from Lairg follows the approximate route of Angus Moray's march to Druim na Coub. Human settlement is very sparse in the interior of Sutherland, roads are usually single track, and distances between shops and filling stations are much greater than is usual in Britain, but with luck and good weather the drive from Inverness to Tongue via Lairg can be done in around three hours. A spectacular panoramic view of the entire area where the battle was fought can be obtained from the layby at Brae Tongue, where a minor road leaves the A836 leading to the village (grid reference NC600560). Carn Fada, identified here as the probable site where the Mackay army deployed, is at grid reference NC566523, about 3 miles south-west of Tongue. The ruins of Castle Varrich provide another good viewpoint for an overview of the area. They overlook the Kyle about half a mile west of the village, and can be reached by a well-marked footpath from Tongue. The original white banner said to have been flown at the battle is in the National Museum of Scotland in Edinburgh, but there is a copy in the excellent Strath Naver Museum at Bettyhill, 12 miles east of Tongue on the A836 in the direction of Thurso.

Chapter 5

Bloody Bay

Date: *c.*1480
Location: At sea off the Isle of Mull, Inner Hebrides
Combatants: John, Lord of the Isles versus MacDonald rebels under Angus Og
Outcome: Rebel victory

In contrast to the situation in the far north, the first seven decades of the fifteenth century were relatively peaceful ones in the Western Isles and the adjacent West Highland mainland. This was at least partly thanks to the hegemony of the MacDonald Lords of the Isles, who although often opposed to the king in Edinburgh had at least attempted to keep some semblance of order among those clans that acknowledged their authority.

Their legal status may have been disputed, but the Lords of the Isles certainly behaved like kings, and made an attempt to govern their possessions accordingly. Grant (1993) points to the large number of charters and other administrative documents that have survived from the era of the MacDonald lords, in contrast to the lack of evidence that their predecessor the Wolf of Badenoch ever devoted much energy to routine government. Another contrast between the two regimes, as James Hunter (1999) points out, was between the Wolf's sinister stronghold at Lochindorb and the unfortified capital of the Lords of the Isles at Finlaggan on the island of Islay. Unlike the Wolf, says Hunter, the latter had no need to fear the people amongst whom they lived. The seventeenth-century chronicler Hugh MacDonald describes the Council of the Isles, which met at Finlaggan, and advised – and in theory elected, or at least approved – the Ri Innse Gall. At its head were four chiefs 'of royal blood': the MacDonalds of Dunyvaig, Clanranald and Keppoch, and MacIain of Ardnamurchan. Next in rank were the four chiefs of major allied clans – the MacLeans of Duart and Lochbuie and the MacLeods of Lewis and Harris – then four lesser allies: the MacNeills of Barra and Gigha, the MacKinnons and the MacQuarries. There were also a number of landowning gentry of lower rank, plus the Bishop of the Isles and the Abbot of Iona. The Council was not a legislative body but it did function as a Supreme Court, hearing appeals against decisions made by the local judges, of whom there was one appointed for each island. Donald Monro, writing around 1549, after the end of the lordship, remarks that 'In thair time thair was great peace and welth in the Iles throw the ministration of justice' (in Martin, 1999). The inauguration of a new lord was no doubt intentionally reminiscent of a royal coronation. It was always presided over by a bishop, with all the leading chiefs in attendance. The lord, dressed in a white habit and carrying his father's sword and a white rod, a symbol of just rule, stood on a stone that had a foot-shaped depression carved into it and placed his own foot in that, signalling that he would walk in the footsteps of his predecessors. Mass was then said and prayers offered for the new ruler, after which feasting would continue for a week. During this time, the lord was expected to make expensive gifts to the monks, bards and musicians. The reputation of the Lords of the Isles as patrons of the arts was carefully promoted, and is remembered in the well-known lament attributed to Gilla Column mac an Ollaimh in the Dean of Lismore's Book, written soon after the fall of the lordship, which concludes, 'There is no joy without Clan Donald': 'Men who are fierce, noble, high-spirited, greatly magnanimous… Their bounty could not be measured, their gifts could not be counted…' (trans. Michael Newton, at www.exploringcelticciv.web.unc.edu, 2016). Nevertheless, their entertainments were not always so intellectual; Martin Martin describes drinking parties at which 'the chief men of the Isles' sat in a circle while the chief's cup-bearer passed around cups of brandy, whisky or similar spirits until everyone was dead drunk, while servants stood by with wheelbarrows to take them home.

The clans that claimed kinship with the Lords of the Isles were numerous and their nomenclature often confusing, so a brief summary (based mainly on the account in Grant, 1952) may be appropriate here. Three early branches of Clan Donald were already in existence before the lordship first appeared in the fourteenth century: the MacAlisters, who held land in Kintyre from the Lords of the Isles, the MacIains of Ardnamurchan, whose fate is described in Chapter 10, and the MacDonalds of Glencoe, descendants of the Angus Og MacDonald who fought at Bannockburn, who remained largely isolated in their wild mountains until they were notoriously massacred by government forces in 1692. The MacDonalds of Clanranald were descended from John, first Lord of the Isles, by his first marriage. They did not inherit the lordship but in compensation received lands in Garmoran, on the rugged mainland coast north of Ardnamurchan. Their headquarters was at Castle Tioram near Acharacle. Sub-branches of Clanranald included those of Moidart, Knoydart (both of these being peninsulas on the west coast) and MacDonell of Glengarry, whose lands were in the hills between Loch Hourn and the Great Glen, the wettest part of the British Isles and one of the most mountainous. A separate branch, MacDonald of Keppoch, was also known as Clanranald of Lochaber. Descended from the second son of the first Lord of the Isles was Clan MacDonald of Dunyvaig and the Glens, also known as Clan Donald South. Their stronghold was Dunyvaig Castle on Islay ('the Glens' refers to their holdings in Antrim, Ireland). The MacDonalds of Lochalsh were based around the sea loch of that name in the north, opposite Skye. They were founded around 1450 by Celestine, a younger son of Alexander, third Lord of the Isles, who had unsuccessfully challenged his brother John of Islay for the lordship. Finally, the MacDonalds of Sleat, or Clan Donald North, traced their ancestry to another son of Alexander, Uisdean or Hugh, who received lands in Sleat on the Isle of Skye from John of Islay. They became one of the most powerful of all the branches, but had to fight constantly against the MacLeods of Dunvegan and their own relatives the Clanranalds, who both had prior claims to the lands that John had given away.

When King James I died in 1437, he was succeeded by his 6-year-old son, James II, on whose behalf Scotland was governed by the earls of Douglas as regents. Under their regime, Alexander, third Lord of the Isles, was released from prison and restored to favour. Not only did he finally receive the earldom of Ross, but in 1439, after the death of the earl of Mar, he became Justiciar of all of Scotland north of the river Forth. He died in 1449 and was followed by his eldest son John, fourth Lord of the Isles. When James II marked his coming of age in 1452 by murdering William, earl of Douglas, whom he accused of conspiring against him with John and the earl of Crawford, the fourth lord joined in the rebellion against the king. However, when the Douglases were finally defeated at the Battle of Arkinholm in 1455, John submitted and was permitted to retain his lands and titles. Then, in 1460, James II was killed by a bursting cannon while trying to recapture Roxburgh Castle, one of the last English possessions left in Scotland after the Wars of Independence, and the kingdom entered another period of uncertainty. The new king, James III, was only two years older than his father had been on his accession, and it was his mother, Mary of Guelders, who took over as regent.

Meanwhile in England, King Edward IV was temporarily victorious in the civil conflict that later became known as the Wars of the Roses, and embarked on a mission to further destabilise his Scottish neighbour.

Edward sent the exiled earl of Douglas to John with an extraordinary proposal that the latter should transfer his allegiance to England in return for an annual cash payment, and that eventually Scotland should be partitioned between Edward, John and the Douglases. It seems surprising that the fourth lord, whom contemporaries regarded as mild mannered and unwarlike, more suited to be a scholar or a clergyman than a war leader, should have agreed to such a risky proposition. Perhaps, as John Roberts (1997) suggests, Donald Balloch, the victor of the Battle of Inverlochy and an inveterate enemy of the

Scottish Crown, was the real driving force behind the negotiations. But in the Treaty of Ardtornish of February 1462, the Lord of the Isles himself agreed to Edward's plan, and John's illegitimate son Angus Og ('Angus the Young') was sent east with an army to take Inverness. King James and his mother knew nothing of the treaty, and although a royal army recaptured Inverness in 1464, John once again managed to make his submission without suffering any serious consequences. He was, presumably, too valuable for his role in maintaining order among the clans to be disposed of as his crimes deserved. He remained in control of both Ross and the Isles until 1476, when in the course of negotiations with England the king finally learned the details of the treasonous deal with Edward. John was summoned to parliament, and being unprepared to fight he had no choice but to comply. Even then he was treated relatively leniently, but the earldom of Ross was confiscated and annexed to the Crown, while he was forced to surrender the title of Lord of the Isles and receive it back as a feudal grant, thus finally establishing in law that he was not an independent ruler but merely a vassal of the king of Scots. This loss of prestige, even more than the territorial losses, infuriated many of John's followers. Among them was Angus Og, who had now emerged as the principal war leader of the MacDonalds.The king had agreed to recognise Angus as John's heir, but it must have seemed to him that all he was set to inherit was a humiliating role as one of James's lackeys. Angus was supported by several of the branches of Clan Donald and their allied clans, and began to act as if he were himself an independent power. Roberts (1997) suggests that Angus rather than John was responsible for several raids carried out by the Islemen around this time, including the seizure of Castle Sween in Knapdale. But John was able to secure a pardon for his errant son, and even arranged a marriage for him with Mary, the daughter of Colin Campbell, the earl of Argyll. Campbell subsequently tried to arrange a meeting on the island of Mull to reconcile John and Angus, but this was not successful. The chronology at this point is unclear, but this may explain why Earl John was apparently present when his supporters clashed with those of his son at Bloody Bay, though he was not in command of the fleet and seems to have played no part in the fighting.

There are good accounts of the Battle of Bloody Bay, based on Hugh MacDonald's work, in Rixson (1998) and Sadler (2010). It is the first naval battle in Hebridean waters about which we have any details since Somerled's epic struggles with Godred of Man in the 1150s (for which see *The Highland Battles*, Chapter 5), and anyone attempting to compare the two must be immediately struck by the difference in scale. We do not have precise numbers for the twelfth-century fleets, but the estimates quoted are consistently much larger than those for Bloody Bay. The 'Chronicle of Man' tells us that at the Epiphany Battle in 1156, Somerled had eighty ships, and as the fight seems to have been inconclusive, we can assume that his opponent was not greatly outnumbered. Two years later, Somerled defeated Godred off the Isle of Man with a fleet of fifty-three ships. But Hugh MacDonald, who lists the commanders and their contingents in the Bloody Bay fight in what appears to be comprehensive detail, mentions only five vessels on the one side versus four on the other (Sadler, 2010). Several suggestions have been made to account for this discrepancy. Sadler suggests that the source mentions only the larger galleys, 'the capital ships of their day', and that both sides would have had 'a shoal of smaller craft riding alongside', contributing to the fight by scouting and perhaps by shooting with small contingents of archers. Denis Rixson (1998), without necessarily discounting this idea, argues that Hebridean sea power really had undergone a decline since its heyday in the early Middle Ages. One possible cause he cites is the general economic decline since the Treaty of Perth, which by breaking the region's links with Norway had disrupted the trade routes between Scandinavia and Ireland, which were once its main source of wealth, and at the same time reduced the incentive to maintain large fleets with which to secure those routes. For similar reasons, good timber for shipbuilding, which had once been imported from Norway, was now much harder to source. Therefore, in Rixson's view, ships had declined in average size as well as in number. For example, in 1545

Donald Dubh took 4,000 men to Ireland in 180 boats, which implies an average of about twenty-two men per vessel. This was admittedly a large fleet, but it was intended purely to transport men and not to fight at sea, so most of these boats would probably have been too small to be effective in a sea battle. In that case, considerable numbers of them could indeed have been present at Bloody Bay, but would have had no significant influence on the fighting and so were not considered worthy of mention.

Various dates between 1480 and 1482 have been suggested for the battle, but Hugh MacDonald tells us that by then, Angus Og and his supporters had finally decided to overthrow his father by force. Angus therefore mustered a fleet with the aim of attacking Mull, but it was delayed on the northern side of the Ardnamurchan Peninsula by unfavourable weather for as long as five weeks. As the strongholds of his principal supporters, the MacDonalds of Sleat and of Clanranald, were respectively on the Isle of Skye and in Moidart, both situated north of Ardnamurchan, it seems reasonable to assume that Angus's presence in the north was aimed at recruiting their fleets to his cause. The Ardnamurchan Peninsula extends westwards from the region of Moidart for about 20 miles, terminating at Ardnamurchan Point, the most westerly location on the British mainland. Still further west lie the islands of Coll and Tiree, and between the point and the collection of reefs and low-lying islets known as the Cairns of Coll is a passage about 6 miles wide. This was a dangerous spot for small wooden ships, exposed to the Atlantic winds, and was traditionally regarded as the boundary between the northern and southern Hebrides. When the winds finally changed, Angus's fleet risked the voyage around the windswept point and made its way east towards the more sheltered waters of Loch Sunart, which separates Ardnamurchan from the neighbouring peninsula of Morvern, with the island of Mull on their right-hand side. The four ships that Hugh mentions as taking part in the battle belonged to Angus himself, Donald Gallich of Sleat, Allan MacRuari the chief of Clanranald, and Allan's son, Ranald Bain. What their strategic aim was is not clear. By this time, they must have been eager for action to break the monotony of shipboard life, but it is quite likely that, as the MacDonald sources imply, the battle came about largely by accident. As they approached the mouth of Loch Sunart, somewhere between Kilchoan on the Ardnamurchan shore and Ardmore Point on the north coast of Mull, Angus's men spotted a galley ahead of them, flying a flag that seemed to be that of their enemies the MacLeans, and immediately advanced to attack it. In fact, the vessel turned out to belong to the Laird of Ardgour, one of MacLean's allies, and when observers on shore noticed the danger it was in, a group of galleys came out from their base on Mull to assist it. Some of them quickly turned back to harbour, fearful of being drawn into a fight with the MacDonalds, but four of them reached Ardgour's vessel and prepared to join battle. According to Hugh MacDonald, they were captained by Hector MacLean of Duart, William MacLeod of Harris, MacNeill of Barra and 'the heir of Torquil of the Lews', in other words, the eldest son of Roderick, chief of the MacLeods of Lewis. (The MacLeods were proud of their descent from Vikings, and their dynasty was known after its semi-legendary founder as the House of Torquil.) The MacNeills claimed to be descended from the legendary Irish hero Niall of the Nine Hostages; their chief at this time appears to have been a certain Roderick, but our sources do not say whether he was present in person at Bloody Bay. Hector MacLean was nicknamed Hector Odhar, which implies a dark complexion, and is described in the MacLean histories as 'brave and warlike'. He held the hereditary post of lieutenant general under the Lord of the Isles, and so we can assume that he was in command of the flotilla.

Hugh does not give the exact location of the battle, but later commentators agree that it was fought in what MacLean (1889) refers to as 'Badh-na-fola, or the Bloody Bay', which is on the north coast of Mull, between Tobermory lighthouse and Ardmore Point. It is possible that the rival fleets moved into the bay to settle the issue by mutual consent, as its relatively sheltered waters would have provided a rather more predictable environment for fighting than the winds and currents of the open loch. Proximity to the shore would also have greatly improved the chances of survival for anyone who fell or was knocked overboard during the fight – something that we know from the Norse sagas was a common occurrence. The harbour mentioned in MacDonald's account must presumably be Tobermory Bay, south of the lighthouse point. The town of Tobermory itself was not in existence at the time, as it was founded as a fishing port in the late eighteenth century, but the bay, which faces east away from the prevailing winds and is further sheltered by Calve Island half a mile offshore, is an obvious refuge for shipping.

As the two fleets slowly closed with each other, the crews straining at the oars, archers stationed on board the galleys would have had ample time to exchange volleys, and Hugh MacDonald tells us that 'Torquil's heir' was struck by two arrows and seriously wounded. His galley was quickly captured 'with all his men', perhaps because they were demoralised by the loss of their leader and agreed to surrender. Then the other galleys came alongside their opponents, preparing for a boarding fight. As Ranald Bain's ship grappled that of MacLeod of Harris, one of Ranald's men, Edmund Mor O'Brien, thrust an oar between the rudder and the stern post of the enemy vessel, jamming the rudder and allegedly preventing it from being steered. This would have had little effect on the course of the boarding action, as the ship could still have been manoeuvred under oars, but it might have made it more difficult for the MacLeod crew to hoist the sail and disengage if they were getting the worst of the encounter. Eventually, Angus Og and Allan of Clanranald joined the fight against the trapped MacLeods, but it seems that they refused to yield and most of them were killed, though according to Hugh MacDonald, their chief was taken alive for ransom. The MacLeod account, however, is rather different (MacLeod, 1927, citing the 'Bannatyne Manuscript'). According to this version, William MacLeod was killed early in the fight and his men began to waver, whereupon a priest who was on board told the clan's standard-bearer to unfurl the famous Fairy Flag of Dunvegan. Seeing this, the men of Lewis, who had previously been fighting on the side of Angus Og, changed sides, but too late to prevent the MacDonald victory. This story seems unlikely, as if the flag had been on the ship it would surely have been captured by the MacDonalds along with its owner. In any case, its magical powers were clearly unsuccessful on this occasion. It was probably at this point that MacNeill of Barra decided that the battle was lost and hoisted sail, fleeing westwards for the open sea. Three of the MacDonald galleys followed in pursuit but were unable to catch him. Hector MacLean apparently struck his colours and surrendered, as he was said to have been captured (MacLean, 1889) during the final stages of the fight, but Earl John, if he was present at all, somehow got away to safety. The Lewis chief was taken to Dunvegan but died there of his wounds.

With his father increasingly sidelined, Angus Og was now the real power in the Isles. According to Hugh MacDonald, he once went so far as to temporarily drive John out of his stronghold at Finlaggan and oblige him to shelter for the night under an upturned boat, though it is not certain whether this humiliation took place before or after the Battle of Bloody Bay. But Angus not only alienated more moderate clansmen by this behaviour, he also dissipated his forces in Easter Ross, in a pointless feud with Clan Mackenzie and several attempts to regain the earldom of Ross. In 1481, he defeated an alliance of eastern clans led by the earl of Atholl and the Mackenzies at Lagabraad near Conon Bridge (though Gregory dates this encounter to before the battle of Bloody Bay), but he succeeded only in obliging the king to send a massive army under the earls of Crawford, Huntly, Argyll and Atholl which drove him back to the west. It was apparently during this campaign that the earl of Atholl captured Angus's infant son, Donald Dubh, provoking a ferocious raid on Atholl by the MacDonalds, in the course of which the earl and countess of Atholl were humiliatingly captured and shipped off to Islay (Gregory). However, Angus's fleet was severely damaged in a storm on the way from Lochaber to Islay and much of his plunder was lost. Gregory believed that Angus took this as a sign of divine displeasure and released the prisoners without even negotiating his son's release in return. But he was not deterred from aggression for long, and in 1490 he was again in occupation of

Inverness, probably in connection with his feud with the Mackenzies. Here he was assassinated in his bed by Diarmaid O'Cairbre, an Irish harper. Four Irish annals report the murder without mentioning any motive, but Hugh MacDonald claims that the harper was in love with the daughter of Kenneth, the son of the Mackenzie chief, and had been promised her hand in return. As it happened, O'Cairbre was captured on the spot by the MacDonalds and put to death by being torn apart by four horses. His severed head was exposed on a stake and became the subject of a famous Gaelic poem in the Dean of Lismore's Book, in which the poet laments the death of Angus, whom he calls the 'King of Islay… ungrudging of gold or silver' (Bingham).

Of the other participants in the battle, Hector Odhar MacLean was imprisoned by Angus Og, but was subsequently ransomed and continued to lead his clan until his death in 1496. The MacNeills had always been regarded as the finest seamen in the Isles, and although they continued to be nominally subject to the MacDonalds, they began to branch out on their own and soon gained a reputation as the most notorious pirates. Allan MacRuari of Clanranald survived to resume a career that was by all accounts disreputable even by the standards of the time. In the course of a lifetime of raiding, which took him as far as Ross and Moray, he was accused of numerous attacks on churches and priests, even on the sacred island of Iona. A hill near the Clanranald stronghold at Castle Tioram known as Tom a'chrodhaidh, or 'the hill of hanging', was remembered in tradition as the place where Allan's victims were often dispatched, among them thirteen captured Mackenzies whose only crime was that their clan had repulsed one of the frequent Clanranald raids on their territory. (This story may relate to the campaign that culminated at Blar na Parc, for which see Chapter 7, in which Allan supported his nominal overlord Alexander MacDonald of Lochalsh against the Mackenzies.) Charles MacDonald (1889) recounts a story that Allan was once intercepted at sea by a fleet of MacLean galleys, but escaped by having himself covered up like a corpse while his piper played a lament. The crew assured the MacLeans that their chief was dead and was being taken to Iona for burial, so, no doubt all too willing to believe the good news, they let the ship go. Allan then doubled back to Mull, where he burnt as many of the MacLeans' houses as he could reach. Despite these depredations, he was reconciled with King James IV in 1495, probably thanks to the influence of his father-in-law, MacIain of Ardnamurchan, but soon returned to his old ways. After he was finally captured and executed by James in 1509, a celebratory poem, preserved like Diarmaid O'Cairbre's in the Dean of Lismore's Book, described the Clanranald chief as a demon, 'worthless' and 'cruel', even to his friends.

Bloody Bay is still named on modern maps, off the coast of Mull just north of Tobermory, approximately at grid reference NM482582. It is not accessible by road, but the eastern end can easily be reached on foot from Tobermory. Take the footpath to the lighthouse, which is signposted on your left as you approach the slipway where the Kilchoan ferry docks; the bay is just beyond the lighthouse, which is a 2km walk from Tobermory along a well-surfaced path. Alternatively, a good view can be obtained from the Tobermory–Kilchoan ferry, and a more distant one from the road from Kilchoan to Ardnamurchan Point on the Ardnamurchan Peninsula itself.

Chapter 6

Massacre and Revenge: Tarbat and Aldicharrish

Date: 11 July 1487
Location: Probably in Strath Oykel, Sutherland
Combatants: Clan Mackay versus Clan Ross
Outcome: Mackay victory

Angus Dubh's successor, Neil Vass Mackay, died around 1460 and was succeeded by his son, Angus Roy, who set out to repair the rift with the Sutherlands by arranging a marriage between his daughter and Sutherland of Dirlot, a prominent member of the family. Unfortunately, thanks to the complicated web of marriage alliances already in existence in the north, in the long run, this succeeded only in adding to the list of the Mackays' enemies. Dirlot was related to the Keith family who had recently acquired land in Caithness, and on account of this tenuous link the Keiths approached Angus Roy asking for his help in their feud with the Gunns, who considered themselves the rightful owners of the land. Why Angus decided to get involved is not clear, but Angus Mackay (1906) speculates that some financial incentive might have been offered by the Keiths, whose chief, Sir Gilbert of Inverugie, had been appointed collector of customs for Strath Naver as well as Caithness and Sutherland. In any case, a large combined army of Mackays, Keiths and MacLeods of Assynt entered Caithness and brought the Gunns to battle at Tannach Moor, near Wick. 'Conflicts of the Clans' dates this fight, which it refers to as Blair-tannie, to 1438, which can hardly be correct as Neil Vass was then in his twenties and had recently escaped from prison, so his son Angus Roy would only have been an infant. A more plausible date of 1464 is given by Sir Robert Gordon. The rest of the account in 'Conflicts of the Clans', however, is the best that we have for the battle. After the usual 'cruel fight, with slaughter on either side', the outnumbered Gunns were overwhelmed and two of their leaders were killed. John Mor MacIain Riabhach of Assynt was named by both this source and Sir Robert Gordon as the man largely responsible for the victory thanks to his heroic actions, which unfortunately are not described in detail. The Keiths subsequently cornered the chief of the Gunns and some of his sons in a chapel and massacred them.

During the Mackays' absence in Caithness, however, a war party of Rosses from Balnagown had attacked and plundered their territory. The Rosses were descended from the original earls of Ross, who, like the Sutherlands, had received the lands and title from King Alexander II in 1234 in recognition of their service against the MacHeth and MacWilliam rebels. By the fifteenth century, the earldom and the clan were separate entities, but the Rosses of Balnagown still had extensive lands bordering on those of the Sutherlands in what is now known as Easter Ross. The dispute between the Mackay and Ross clans may have had its origins as long ago as the aftermath of Druim na Coub. According to Angus Mackay, after the deaths of Angus Moray and his two sons in that battle, the Rosses managed to come into possession of lands they had owned at Edderton and Kincardine, near the shores of the Dornoch Firth. However, the victorious Strath Naver Mackays also laid claim to them, leading to a feud that disturbed the north for several decades. Both sides are regularly accused by historians of raiding the other, so that it is impossible to establish who started the fighting, but Angus Roy quickly took the initiative and subjected the Ross country to a long series of damaging incursions. In 1486, he led a raid that swept across the county as far as Tarbat, the site of the modern village of Portmahomack near the north-eastern tip of the Tarbat Peninsula. Angus must have been extremely confident in his military superiority to have advanced so far east, because the narrow peninsula was an obvious place to trap an invader, but it was here, with an army under Alexander Ross of Balnagown closing in on them, that Angus and his men were forced to seek sanctuary in the church.

Churches, being among the very few substantial stone structures in many parts of the Highlands, were commonly used as refuges in this way by outnumbered armed forces, but the sanctity of the buildings was seldom respected by their enemies, and the fact that they generally had thatched roofs was an irresistible temptation to arsonists. In fact, the ancient Viking tradition of hall burning continued throughout the Middle Ages, and there are numerous traditions of people – sometimes war parties, as here, but all too often innocent non-combatants – being trapped and burned to death in churches. Neither Mackay nor Ross sources tell us very much about what happened to Angus Roy and his men, but John Ross (1968) quotes a poem that alleged that forty Mackays were killed or wounded outside the building, perhaps by a surprise attack, and the rest penned up inside the church, with Ross axemen guarding the doors. The church was then set on fire and the remaining Mackays, including Angus Roy, were all burnt to death. As his namesake (Mackay, 1906) reports, neither the king nor the Scottish Church took any action in response to this sacrilege. James III had recently survived an attempt by his brother, Alexander, duke of Albany, to take over the government, but his position remained insecure. He seldom left Edinburgh and concentrated his energies mainly on making peace with England, so that his writ scarcely ran in the far north. He was to be killed during or shortly after the Battle of Sauchieburn near Stirling in June 1488, by rebels loyal to his son, the future James IV.

It was therefore left to the Mackays to take their own revenge. Angus Roy was succeeded by his eldest son, Iye Roy of Strath Naver, but the initiative for the subsequent moves against the Rosses seems to have come from Angus's second son, John Riabhach, and William Dubh Aberich, son of Iain Aberach, the victor of Druim na Coub. Once again, the MacLeods of Assynt took the side of the Mackays. According to Sir Robert Gordon, John Mackay also approached Earl John of Sutherland, 'upon whom he depended', and asked for help in avenging his father's murder. The earl, we are told, sent him a company of men under his uncle, Robert Sutherland. However, Angus Mackay (1906) disputes this account, arguing that although there may have been a brief period of détente between the Mackays and the Sutherlands at this period, Gordon is an unreliable source as he 'never forgets his self-imposed task of magnifying the House of Sutherland', and that the idea that the latter was the feudal superior of the Mackays 'nowhere existed save in his own fertile imagination'. Angus Mackay also points out that Earl John was married to a daughter of the Ross chief and was unlikely to have agreed to help to destroy his own father-in-law, and also that the judicial review into the subsequent events which was held in 1494 made no mention of the involvement of the Sutherlands. However, Gordon does add one extra detail, which tends to support the idea that there were Sutherlands present at the Battle of Aldicharrish. It is especially worthy of note as he has no obvious motive for mentioning it, since it is very much to the credit of the Mackays, whom he is usually at pains to belittle. After the battle, says Sir Robert, the Assynt men who were with the Mackay army proposed to William Dubh Aberich that they should conspire to cheat the Sutherland contingent out of its share of the spoils, but William angrily refused, threatening to be an enemy to anyone who behaved in such a 'fraudulent and base' manner. According to Gunn and Mackay, he then alerted the Sutherland men and advised them to stand to arms until the Mackays could deploy to protect them, thus gaining a reputation for fair play even towards his hereditary enemies.

Exactly where the battle took place is not certain. Sir Robert Gordon says that the Mackays invaded Strath Oykel and Ross of Balnagown marched to meet them at a place called Auldicharish, 'upon which a most severe conflict ensued'. 'Conflicts of the Clans' places 'Aldicharrish' in Strath Carron, the neighbouring valley to the south, and it seems likely that both these locations were attacked at various times during the campaign. One interpretation (see the Wikipedia article on 'The Battle of Aldy Charrish') links the site to the stream known as Allt a'Charraigh, which flows into the Kilmachalmack

Burn, a tributary of the river Oykel. This would place it on the northern slopes of the hills overlooking Strath Oykel from the south, a logical place to intercept an army ravaging the farms in the valley, but there have been no excavations to confirm this identification. Allt a'Charraigh translates as 'The Stream of the Rock', where 'carraig' is a large prominent rock such as might be used as a lookout post or for fishing, but even if such a feature could be located in the area it would not necessarily pinpoint the spot where the fighting took place. It is perhaps noteworthy that it is within a few miles of the better-known site of the Battle of Tuiteam Tarbhach in 1406, where the Mackays caught and annihilated a MacLeod raiding party. The same handful of routes across the country were used repeatedly by raiding armies, and because the spots at which the terrain permitted them to be intercepted were relatively few, battles tended to cluster around these locations. The brief account in 'Conflicts of the Clans' describes the battle as a 'cruel and furious combat, which continued a long space, with incredible obstinacy' until at last the Ross warriors, 'being unable to endure or resist the enemy's forces, were utterly disbanded and put to flight'. This of course is the traditional formula for such descriptions, but it is given some credibility by the casualty list. Apart from Alexander Ross of Balnagown, the defeated Rosses lost seventeen 'landed gentlemen' or '*daoine uasile*', of whom 'Conflicts of the Clans', quoting Sir Robert Gordon, names seven, as well as 'a great number' of common soldiers. Gordon says that the outcome of the fight was in doubt for a long time, but that eventually the men of Ross gave way 'after great slaughter was made among them'. The implication is perhaps that on this occasion the Mackay victory was achieved not by the sort of clever tactics or manoeuvres that had been associated with the career of Iain Aberach, but purely by attrition, wearing down the enemy and gradually picking off their leaders in a frontal slogging match.

The Mackays followed up their victory by raiding the Ross country as far east as Tain on the Dornoch Firth, not only taking their revenge for the massacre at Tarbat but enriching themselves with great herds of captured cattle, which they drove back to Strath Naver. The Mackay-

Ross feud nevertheless continued to flare up, and in 1493, the former launched a second armed raid, which the Rosses appear not to have been able to resist, and which netted another great haul of livestock, said to have amounted to 1,200 cattle, 100 horses and 1,000 sheep and goats. This time the victims complained to the Crown, and a court judgement dated July 1501, cited by Angus Mackay, awarded them 6,000 marks in damages, although there is no record that they ever received the money. During the reign of James IV, the dispute gradually lost its ferocity as both parties managed to prosper. The Rosses applied for and received royal charters confirming them in the possession of most of their lands, and the Mackays escaped further punishment by resuming their tradition of service to the monarchy. In 1503, Donald Dubh, the son of Angus Og and grandson of John, the last Lord of the Isles, escaped from prison, where he had been languishing since the aftermath of Bloody Bay (Chapter 5), and fled to the isle of Lewis. There he found support from Torquil, the chief of the MacLeods of the island, and others who were unhappy about James's centralising policies. It required three expeditions between 1503 and 1506 to suppress Torquil and return Donald Dubh to custody. In the latter year, the earl of Huntly collected a fleet of ships from Edinburgh with which he transported a predominantly Mackay army to Stornoway, where it assisted in the successful siege of the castle. Munro and Cameron sources mention another event during this period of which the details are obscure, and which seems to have been omitted from the Mackay histories. A Cameron army operating in support of Donald Dubh is said to have marched as far north as Achnashellach in Wester Ross, where it ambushed and defeated an army of Mackays and Munros, killing William Munro of Foulis (Drummond, 1842; Mackenzie, 1898). Despite this setback, Iye Roy Mackay was well rewarded for his loyalty to the Crown, at last being granted charters for the lands of Strath Naver, Strath Halladale and Assynt, among others.

The village of Portmahomack (grid reference NH914840) in Easter Ross is the site of Tarbat Old Church (now the Tarbat Discovery Centre), where the massacre of the Mackays took place. The church has been partially rebuilt several times since 1486, most recently in 1756, but it stands on a very ancient site and a great deal of archaeological work has been carried out here recently. It is open to the public, and in the crypt can be seen the marks of a fire that may well date from the fight in which Angus Roy and his men died. If this is the case, it is a possibly unique example of traces of medieval clan battle still being visible today. The Allt a'Charraigh is approximately at grid reference NH480968, but the area is now a forestry plantation and there is nothing to be seen on the ground today. It is, however, possible to drive the length of Strath Oykel along the A837, which leaves the A836 Bonar Bridge to Lairg road near Carbisdale Castle (grid reference NH574955). (Carbisdale Castle itself, despite its spectacular location overlooking the Kyle of Sutherland, is not medieval but was erected in the early twentieth century.) The site of the Battle of Tuiteam Tarbhach is near where the A837 crosses the Tutim Burn at grid reference NC436015.

Chapter 7

'A Man's Work': Blar Na Parc

Date: *c.*1491
Location: Near Strathpeffer, Easter Ross
Combatants: Clan MacDonald versus Clan Mackenzie
Outcome: Mackenzie victory

The name Mackenzie derives from the Gaelic MacCoinneach, or son of Kenneth, and the first Kenneth Mackenzie known to history was a vassal of the earl of Ross, who in 1267 was already occupying the castle of Eilean Donan, at the mouth of Loch Duich in Kintail, on the mainland of Wester Ross. During the Wars of Independence, the Mackenzies of Kintail had supported Robert the Bruce, who is said to have once taken refuge at Eilean Donan (Dunlop, 1953), and afterwards they continued their policy of loyalty to the monarchy, although they joined the MacDonalds for the Harlaw campaign in 1411, perhaps feeling that they had no option in view of the overwhelming force that the invaders brought into the area. For many years, they had pursued a feud with the earls of Ross in an attempt to secure their independence, but when in the fifteenth century the earldom came into the possession of the MacDonalds, the Mackenzies found themselves vassals of the Lords of the Isles. This placed them in a difficult position since the MacDonalds were frequently in rebellion against the Crown. When James I arrested the clan leaders in 1427, the Mackenzie chief, Alexander, was still a child, so he was sent not to prison but to school in Perth, where he received a good education in Lowland ways and was confirmed in his support for the king, so that he earned the nickname of 'Ionraic', 'The Just' or 'The Upright'. Several stories suggest that he acted as an unofficial royal agent in maintaining law and order in the north. At one point he is said to have led 600 men into Sutherland, where he thwarted an invasion by the Mackays, who had taken advantage of the fact that the earl of Sutherland was absent at court. Little is known of the rest of Alexander's life, but two royal charters, dated 1463 and 1477, confirmed his possession of lands in Kintail and in Strath Conan, Strath Bran and Strath Garve in Easter Ross. It seems that the Mackenzies had already extended their power to the east before this date, because Alexander is also mentioned in connection with strongholds at Kinellan, near Strathpeffer, and Brahan, which is near Dingwall. Matheson (2014) suggests that his ancestors had been granted Kinellan by Sir Walter Leslie, who was earl of Ross in the 1370s, as a means of splitting the Mackenzies and bringing one branch under his control. This meant that the clan now occupied some of the best agricultural land in northern Scotland, a stark contrast with the mountainous west coast and significant addition to their wealth and power.

After the death of Angus Og in 1490 (see Chapter 5), his father, John of the Isles, named as his successor his nephew, Alexander MacDonald of Lochalsh, who controlled the lands of Lochalsh, Lochcarron and Lochbroom in Wester Ross which he had inherited from his father, Celestine. He also inherited Angus Og's feud with the Mackenzies, which with hindsight seems to have been a particularly pointless distraction from the real problems facing the lordship. The traditional account of how this feud arose is given by Mackenzie (1894). When his eldest son, Kenneth, reached adulthood, Alexander Mackenzie arranged a marriage for him with Margaret, the daughter of his overlord, John of the Isles. The marriage was not happy, and was a cause of trouble from the beginning. Alexander of Lochalsh invited his cousin Margaret and her husband to stay with him for Christmas, but Kenneth arrived without his wife, and not content with this insult he had an argument with MacLean of Duart, with whom he was already on bad terms, about his lodgings. Kenneth ended up having to leave the house in a hurry and stay with a neighbouring tenant, an experience that left him so humiliated that he persuaded his host to adopt the name of Mackenzie, so that it should not be said that he had been forced to take refuge with a stranger. He returned to his father's house at Kinellan, but soon afterwards received a message from Alexander MacDonald, who obviously still regarded himself as the lawful owner of the place, ordering Kenneth and his father to leave at once. Lady Margaret, the message pointedly added, was welcome to remain. We do not know whose side Margaret actually took in the argument, but Kenneth flew into a rage and threw her out of the house, repudiating the marriage and telling her to go back to the MacDonalds. Margaret was blind in one eye, and her husband added insult to injury by sending her back riding on a one-eyed horse, accompanied by a one-eyed servant and a one-eyed dog. Only a few days later, Kenneth went to his neighbour Fraser of Lovat and demanded the hand of his daughter Agnes, which might of course point to the real motive behind his bad relations with his previous wife. Despite the menacing presence of numerous Mackenzie henchmen camped outside his house, Lovat insisted that he would only agree if Agnes consented, which she did with suspicious alacrity. The couple went back to Kinellan, and in Alexander Mackenzie's words, 'ever after they lived together as husband and wife'. Agnes's uncle happened to be the Bishop of Ross, and he eventually obtained from the Pope a decree legitimising the 'marriage' and all the couple's children. Meanwhile, MacDonald of Lochalsh was so furious that he immediately set about raising an army to avenge the insult to his clan. This version of course may or may not be true, and even if it is, it is not the whole story. The lands that Alexander Mackenzie had been given in Easter Ross in 1477 were among those confiscated from the Lord of the Isles when he forfeited the earldom of Ross after the discovery of the Treaty of Ardtornish, so it was inevitable that the Mackenzies would eventually be drawn into conflict with anyone attempting to restore the fortunes of the lordship.

MacLean (1889) and Mackenzie (1894 & 1898) provide detailed accounts of the ensuing campaign, based mainly on Mackenzie and

MacDonald sources. Alexander 'The Upright' was around 90 years old and infirm by this time, or possibly had already died, leaving command of the clan in the hands of Kenneth, who would become known to history as Coinneach a'bhlair, or Kenneth of the Battle. Several local and allied clans rallied to his standard. The MacRaes were a small clan with a formidable reputation as archers (see Chapter 3), who had been close allies of the Mackenzies since the fourteenth century, when both clans were living in Kintail. They seem to have served the Mackenzie chiefs as hereditary soldiers and bodyguards, hence their nickname of 'Mackenzie's coat of mail'. Another minor local clan, the MacLennans, were traditionally employed as standard-bearers. Alexander MacDonald marched up the Great Glen and then turned eastwards into Badenoch and Strathspey, aiming for Inverness. He probably had around 1,500 men – his own MacDonalds from Lochalsh, plus Clanranalds, MacIains, MacLeans and Camerons, whose chief Ewen was related to him by marriage. Near their objective, they were joined by reinforcements from Clan Chattan and some of the Frasers of Lovat, though others of that clan later joined the opposite side. In view of Lord Lovat's somewhat irregular new relationship with Kenneth Mackenzie, it is likely that he was trying to hedge his bets and ensure his survival whichever side was victorious. Since their defeat by the Mackays at Poul an Tarie (Chapter 4), the Mathesons had split into northern and southern branches, which also fought on opposite sides.

The invaders took the castle at Inverness without difficulty, and then began to launch raids into Mackenzie territory. After ravaging the Black Isle and Strath Conan and driving off thousands of cattle and sheep from the Sheriff of Cromarty's lands, they arrived at Contin, near the modern town of Strathpeffer, on a Sunday morning. The men of fighting age had already been called up to join the Mackenzie army, which was mustering only about a mile away near Loch Kinellan. A small island in the loch, measuring 76 metres by 36 and now overgrown with bushes, was identified by early twentieth-century archaeologists as a crannog, or artificial island (www.canmore.org.uk). These features are common in Scotland and were built as refuges from as early as the Iron Age, but the earliest dateable finds from this site were fourteenth or fifteenth century. The Canmore website states that it was used as a hunting lodge by the earls of Ross, and that Kenneth Mackenzie occupied it as a secure base before the Battle of Blar na Parc. It is unlikely that he would have failed to take advantage of such an obvious asset, but he still had only 600 men there to face three times that number of the enemy, and he seems to have been undecided about whether he could successfully resist them. Reinforcements, however, continued to trickle in to his camp. Alexander Mackenzie tells how the night before the battle, a neighbour, Brodie of Brodie, had been passing through Kinellan, and seeing the Mackenzies preparing for combat he offered to stay and help. A blacksmith belonging to the Frasers of Lovat had also collected some friends and was leading them to help the Mackenzies. On that Sunday, the church at Contin was filled with the noncombatants – old men, women, children, and the priest, 'thinking themselves secure within its precincts from any enemy professing Christianity', as Alexander Mackenzie (1894) puts it. But Alexander MacDonald locked them in, placed guards on the doors and set fire to the church, burning to death all those inside. Even by the standard of the time this was an appalling act; we have seen, among other examples, how the Mackays were similarly killed in a burning church at Portmahomack, but they were at least enemy fighting men and not innocent civilians. MacDonald's motive is not clear. Alexander Mackenzie says that he had 'little or no scruples on the score of religion', and he may simply have been seeking a way to avenge the insult that he had received from the Mackenzies, but the atrocity had an immediate effect on the morale of the defenders. Some of the villagers who had been outside the church hurried to inform Kenneth, while others drove their cattle into the hills to prevent them from being stolen by the invaders. The Mackenzie leader 'expressed his gratitude that the enemy… had now engaged God against them by their impious conduct' (Mackenzie, 1894), and resolved to stand and fight where he was rather than expose any more of the clan territory to destruction.

Being so greatly outnumbered, Kenneth took up a defensive position near Loch Kinellan at a place known as Parc, or 'The Park', a name that perhaps referred to a deer park surrounding the hunting lodge. He deployed his small army on a hill behind a stretch of low-lying boggy ground into which he hoped to lure the invaders. The Highland Historic Environment Record website locates the battle site at grid reference NH 4732 5689, about 1,500 metres north-east of Contin and 400 metres west of the A834. According to clan tradition, the elderly chief of the Mackenzies, Alexander, was sent for safety to the stronghold of the Raven's Rock near Strathpeffer, to which Kenneth planned to retire if he was forced to abandon his position. About midday, Alexander MacDonald and his men appeared on a rise on the opposite side of the bog; this was probably the low hill marked on the OS map as 128 metres in height, south-west of the battle site and on the direct line of approach from Contin. It seems that the MacDonalds were not expecting the Mackenzies to make a stand, and Alexander Mackenzie says that they initially deployed into line of battle so that their chief could review them, rather than with any idea of having to fight. Kenneth, observing from the slightly lower rise on the north side of the bog, put his plan into action without delay. He placed a group of archers in ambush on one flank, led by his brother Duncan, and then led the Mackenzie main body forward into the swamp, making use of paths and strips of drier ground known only to the local clansmen. On the far side, Alexander saw them coming and laughed at 'Mackenzie's impudent madness', to which his older and wiser lieutenant Gillespie MacLean replied that when an opponent behaved with such boldness it was best to be wary in case he was planning some stratagem. Alexander, regarding his attitude as cowardice, responded that for all he cared Gillespie could join the Mackenzies, and the MacDonalds would make breakfast of the lot of them.

But then the rest of the MacLean contingent, led by Lachlan MacThearlaich of Lochbuie, saw the enemy approaching in apparent confusion and charged recklessly towards them into the bog. Kenneth and his men fell back fighting, luring them deeper into the worst of the mire, and when they were sufficiently disordered Duncan sprang his ambush. His archers threw the floundering MacLeans into confusion with volleys of arrows before charging in to scatter them in a brief flurry of close-quarter fighting, and then rapidly pressing on to outflank the MacDonald main body. As MacLean (1889) says that Kenneth Mackenzie then turned and attacked the enemy's right with 'furious impetuosity', we can assume that Duncan was advancing from their left, and so was deployed on the Mackenzie right wing. Suddenly facing envelopment by an opponent whom they must have assumed was already in full retreat, the MacDonalds hardly had time to deploy to face the new threat before they found themselves having to fall back in their turn. But their army did not disintegrate at once, and several desperate attempts were made to halt the Mackenzies' advance. Gillespie MacLean, stung by the insult he had received from his commander, led a small group of picked fighters to try to kill Kenneth himself, and he cut down numerous Mackenzies as he fought his way towards where the chief was urging on his men in the thickest of the battle. Kenneth, who the MacLean sources admit was Gillespie's equal in courage and by far his superior in strength, saw him coming and signalled to him to come forward and meet him in single combat. Gillespie hesitated for a moment, so the Mackenzie chief decided not to stand on ceremony but rushed at him and cut off his arm with a single blow. The MacLean champion fell dead on the spot. At this point Kenneth noticed his standard-bearer, a MacLennan, fighting like an ordinary warrior, without the standard, which had been entrusted to him. When asked where the flag was, he replied that he had left the MacDonalds' standard-bearer guarding it. It turned out that the two men had encountered each other in the battle, and MacLennan had killed the other by thrusting his flag staff, which presumably had some sort of spearhead on the shaft, through his body. Being unable to extract it, he had left some of his men to look after it and thrown himself back into the fray.

Quoting another Mackenzie tradition, MacLean goes on to tell how Lachlan MacThearlaich met his death. As the battle was about to be joined, one of the leaders on the Mackenzie side, Kenneth's half-brother Hector Roy, saw a certain Duncan from Kintail, whom other traditions describe as a member of the MacRae clan, an 'ungainly but powerful looking' young man who was wandering rather aimlessly about, and asked him what he was looking for. He had no armour and was equipped only with a rusty old axe, which he had apparently found lying around, perhaps discarded by a wealthier warrior. No doubt frustrated by his lack of proper equipment, he replied, 'Unless I get a man's esteem, I shall not perform a man's work.' After being assured that if he did his bit he would be suitably rewarded, he ran into the thick of the fight, killed a man, dragged the body out and sat down on it. Hector spotted him and again asked what he thought he was doing. This time the reply was that in exchange for one man's wages he would do one man's work, and that he had already done that by killing an enemy. Hector told him that he would receive two men's rewards if he killed another, so Duncan rushed off again and did so, bringing this body too back to his growing pile and sitting down on it. An exasperated Hector must have realised by now that he was dealing with a rather challenging character, so he simply said, 'Do your best and we shall not be reckoning with you.' At this Duncan seems to have finally understood what was expected of him, because he threw himself into the fight and began to cut down the MacDonalds 'like grass' with his rusty axe, until Lachlan MacThearlaich intercepted him and the two men faced each other in single combat. From the detailed account of the fight that has survived – assuming of course that there is any truth in it – it appears that at least some of their comrades must have stopped fighting themselves to watch the epic duel. In contrast to his unprotected opponent, Lachlan was clad in full mail armour and helmet, and he had a reputation as an experienced warrior, so few observers can have had much doubt about the outcome. But the younger and more lightly equipped MacRae was able to avoid his enemy's blows as he slowly fell back in front of him, until he reached the edge of a ditch. Lachlan, thinking that he had him cornered, aimed another blow at him, but Duncan jumped backwards across the ditch and his opponent stumbled forward. Making another wild swing, Lachlan again missed and got his blade stuck in the soft earth on the far side of the ditch; he bent forward to extract it and briefly exposed the back of his neck beneath his helmet. Duncan did not miss his opportunity, but decapitated the MacLean with a single blow. This feat earned him the nickname of Donnchadh Mor na Tuaighe, or Big Duncan of the Axe. Dixon (1886) tells how Duncan presented himself to Kenneth Mackenzie after the battle with four enemy heads and demanded to know whether he had earned his supper, which he was duly given. According to the same author, he was in action again in 1501 at the Battle of Knockfarrel or Drumchatt, where 140 Mackenzies are said to have destroyed an army of Dingwalls, Munros and others that outnumbered them five to one. Brodie of Brodie had also fought bravely in the battle and was said to have been badly wounded, but he insisted on continuing his journey the next day. As a result of his action the Mackenzies and the Brodies became firm friends, a relationship that outlasted most of the fickle clan loyalties of the time.

On learning of the death of Lachlan, the MacDonalds finally lost heart and began to flee the field, but the Mackenzies pursued ruthlessly and killed most of them. When they reached the banks of the river Conon, about 2 miles from the battlefield, some 300 of them tried to rally, but Kenneth followed them up and dispersed them, taking Alexander MacDonald and his son prisoner. According to 'Conflicts of the Clans', many more of the MacDonalds were drowned 'in the river of Connan', and Alexander Mackenzie reports a tradition that they met their deaths at Moy, about 2 miles south-east of Contin, as a result of the quick thinking of an old woman who lived there. On arriving at the river, the fugitives asked her if there was a ford, to which she replied that although the whole stretch of river looked deep it was in fact safe to cross. Needless to say, this was not true, and the MacDonalds who tried to do it were knocked off their feet by the current. They grabbed at the bushes along the bank, but the woman and her companions cut these away with their sickles, so that the men were unable to pull themselves out and were swept to their deaths. The blacksmith from Lovat and his party were late for the battle, and by the time they arrived at the Conon, the MacDonalds were already in flight. They therefore stationed themselves on the far bank to intercept those few who managed to get across, and were said to have killed every one of them.

Alexander of Lochalsh and his son were taken back to Kinellan, but within six months, Kenneth released them in return for their word of honour – which naturally was not kept – never to attack the Mackenzies again. Very soon after that, in February 1492, Kenneth died of unknown causes. Mackenzie (1894) quotes the seventeenth-century writer George Mackenzie, first earl of Cromarty, to the effect that despite his sudden rise to fame and power as result of the battle, Kenneth had been a good neighbour to the other clans of Easter Ross and a just master to his dependents. His behaviour towards Lady Margaret was reprehensible, but in all other matters, 'he merits justly to be numbered amongst the best of our Scots patriots'. He was succeeded by his son by his first wife, also Kenneth, who seems to have been murdered in mysterious circumstances about seven years later, and then by another son, John 'of Killin', whose mother was Agnes of Lovat, and who was still very young. This left power in the hands of the boys' tutor, their uncle Hector Roy, under whom the clan's reputation as dependable supporters of the Crown was somewhat tarnished. After their victory at Blar na Parc the Mackenzies launched a series of brutal raids to punish the MacDonalds and their allies, which caused so much damage on the Black Isle that the news of it reached Edinburgh, and George Gordon, the second earl of Huntly, who was then Lieutenant of the North, had to be sent to restore order. Hector Roy had also been carving out a power base for himself in Gairloch, in Wester Ross, where he had arranged a marriage between his sister and a local gentleman, Allan MacLeod. This threat so alarmed the MacLeods of Lewis that they murdered Allan and his sons. The government was then persuaded to grant Hector a Commission of

Fire and Sword against the murderers, which he executed with such excessive zeal that he drove the MacLeods out of Gairloch altogether. Gregory (1836) quotes government documents which show that the blame for the disturbances was placed squarely on Hector, whom they describe as provoking feuds with the MacLeods, Munroes and others, and as being 'obnoxious to the government as a disturber of the public peace'. In 1499, Huntly led an army of 3,000 men against the Mackenzies, who were by then being described as 'the King's rebels', but he did not manage to apprehend Hector, who escaped to Eilean Donan Castle. There he remained until 1511, rejecting John of Killin's claim on the grounds that his parents' marriage was not legitimate, and keeping the rents from the area for himself. John eventually raised his own supporters, secured recognition from King James IV as the rightful chief and forced Hector to come to terms. The two men were reconciled and fought side by side at Flodden two years later, though according to Alister Farquhar Matheson, the Mackenzies of Gairloch continued to oppose their own clan chiefs when the opportunity arose, and frequently gave their support to the various sixteenth-century revolts of the MacDonalds.

In 1493, James III's successor, James IV, reached the age of 18 and began to take the government of Scotland into his own hands. Although there was no proof that John Lord of the Isles had been personally responsible for the Blar na Parc campaign, the continual violence in the north had finally exasperated the government. No doubt, the king considered that even if John was entirely innocent, his inability to control the Islemen removed any justification for allowing him to retain his exceptional status. One of James's first acts was to declare the lordship forfeit and annex all its remaining lands to the Crown. John, who no longer had an army on which he could rely, had no choice but to acquiesce. He was taken to court and given a small pension, but he died in obscurity in Dundee in 1503, the last of the Lords of the Isles.

The battle site at Blar na Parc is in the vicinity of Loch Kinellan, roughly at grid reference NH472569, but it has not been located more precisely. The Canmore website places it in what is now an improved and partially drained field south of the loch, but notes that metal detector surveys have failed to find any artefacts that would confirm this, although Bronze Age axe heads have been recovered from the area. The loch can be reached via a narrow side road on the left as you approach Strathpeffer on the A834 from Contin, signposted 'Loch Kinellan Walks'. There is parking available near the Korean War memorial on the lochside, and a path leads westwards along the shore towards the woods at the far end. The battle was fought either in the fields on your left, or possibly in front in what is now a wooded area, separated from the western end of the loch by a low ridge. The present parish church at Contin is on the site of the chapel burnt by the MacDonalds before the battle. The present building dates mainly from the eighteenth century, but the Historic Environment Scotland website suggests that the 'main walls' at least follow the outline of those rebuilt in the 1490s, immediately after the destruction.

Chapter 8

Disaster at Flodden

James IV would survive John of the Isles by only a decade. In 1502 he had signed an optimistically titled Treaty of Perpetual Peace with Henry VII of England, but when Henry VIII succeeded his father in 1509, relations between the two countries quickly deteriorated, thanks largely to Henry's insistence on being recognised as James's overlord. When England joined the coalition against France in the war of the League of Cambrai and Henry led his army to besiege Thérouanne in Artois, James tried to persuade him to withdraw, but was rebuffed. So in August 1513, the Scots invaded Northumberland with an army that may have been as large as 40,000 men. The immediate pretext was the Scottish claim that 'the bastard' Heron, an illegitimate son of a prominent Northumberland family, had murdered Robert Kerr, the Warden of the Scottish East March on the border, and had been given asylum in England. Not only was this the biggest Scottish army ever sent against England, it was also the most modern. James had assembled a train of heavy artillery, equipped the Lowland spearmen with the new 18-foot pikes which were in vogue in Europe, and ensured that as many of his men as possible were protected by plate armour. Contingents were summoned from all over the kingdom, and it is an indication of the authority of the monarchy at this time that all but the most intransigent of the Highland clans were represented, though their fighting men were not re-equipped but fought with their traditional bows, swords and axes. Among the most important contingents were the Gordons, Grants, Mackenzies, MacLeans, Campbells and Mackays; even the MacDonalds were there, led by Iain MacIain of Ardnamurchan. In the absence of King Henry, his wife Katherine of Aragon was acting as regent in England,

and she acted decisively, sending an army 26,000 strong, raised mainly from the north and midlands and led by the veteran earl of Surrey. Like the Highlanders, these men were still armed with bows and bills in medieval fashion, though they preferred reinforced jacks and plate armour to coats of mail, and although Surrey possessed some light cannon, they were not considered to be a match for James's artillery. But events were to conspire to negate all of the Scots' apparent advantages.

James quickly captured the castles south of the border at Norham and Etal as well as Ford, the stronghold of the Heron family, but remained passively at Ford instead of advancing on Berwick-upon-Tweed, a decision that was allegedly influenced by the charms of the Lady Heron. On Surrey's approach, the king dug in on the commanding ridge of Flodden Edge to await the English attack. Surrey tried to induce him to move by proposing battle by mutual consent on level ground nearby, but James refused to take the bait, arguing that it was not fitting for a king to obey a summons from a mere earl. So Surrey decided on a bold outflanking manoeuvre, assisted by the local knowledge provided by 'the bastard' Heron, who had been pardoned by Katherine and sent to join the army. The English marched around the Scottish position and cut its communications, forcing James to take up another position on a hill further north, overlooking the village of Branxton. Here, in the afternoon of 9 September 1513, the battle was fought. Two of the three 'battles' that comprised the English force were drawn up on Piper Hill in front of the Scottish position, but the third, under Sir Edward Stanley, was the last to leave camp and would not arrive until the evening. The solid pike blocks were drawn up in the Scottish centre, with the more lightly armed Highlanders on the wings.

An initial artillery duel was inconclusive, though the Scottish guns failed to perform as expected because of their slow rate of fire, and because in their hastily adopted new location they had not been sited where they could command a sufficiently good field of fire. The psychological effect of the cannonade on the Highlanders must have been considerable, though they probably suffered few casualties from it, as the English guns seem to have concentrated against the densely packed pikemen in the centre. Then the Scottish left wing, consisting of Hume's borderers alongside Gordons and other clansmen from the central Highlands led by Alexander Gordon, the third earl of Huntly, charged down the hill and up into the English positions. They possessed two advantages that their comrades on the rest of the front lacked. Most if not all of the borderers seem to have fought as pikemen like the other Lowland contingents, but they had the support of the more mobile Highlanders with their swords and bows, who could guard their flanks and intervene against the flanks of the enemy when the main bodies clashed. This role was performed in the European armies that James had tried to emulate by crossbowmen, halberdiers or men armed with sword and buckler, but these troop types were absent from the rest of the army. Also the valley between the two hills was more shallow here than on the Scottish right and centre, and the ground across which the Scots charged was well above the water table, so that they avoided the bogs that lay in wait to trap their comrades. Huntly's men drove the English back in disorder, but the victors failed to exploit the situation, allegedly thanks to the treachery or cowardice of Hume, who argued that by defeating the men opposite them his borderers had done their bit. So Huntly recalled his Highlanders to their standards, regrouping at leisure while James launched his main body against Surrey's centre.

At first, the phalanxes of Scottish pikemen seemed unstoppable, as the nobles who marched in their front ranks were so well armoured that even the arrows of the famous English longbows could not hurt them. But according to Younger's analysis (2012), James's up-to-date army was doomed by events that had taken place thousands of years earlier. Branxton Hill, where the Scots were deployed, consisted of hard, poorly drained soils that had originated as mud piled up by glacial action during the Ice Age, while the English on Piper Hill were standing on sand and gravel, which was much better drained. James's scouts had not had time to reconnoitre the ground in front of their new position, and he did not realise the significance of the fact that as the valley deepened from left to right, the surface fell below the level of the water table, which Younger calculates at being around 75 metres above sea level. So at the bottom of Branxton Hill lay a stretch of waterlogged ground, fed by groundwater seepage and by runoff from the muddy slopes above, which was more extensive on the Scottish side and in which the heavily armoured pikemen quickly became mired. The pike was a decisive weapon if it could be deployed properly, but it had to be used in dense close order formations so that the men could support each other and prevent an enemy getting past the spearheads and attacking them at close range. This required firm open ground in order to maintain the momentum, and when halted and thrown into disorder the men were encumbered by their long and unwieldy weapons and unable to defend themselves. They were gradually cut to pieces by the more mobile English billmen, who either still held their positions on the dry ground or could easily retreat to it to regroup if they were hard-pressed. Younger states that the area where most of the Scottish casualties occurred 'corresponds precisely' to the groundwater seepage zone. James joined the fight in person but was killed alongside most of his nobles, who because of their superior armour had been concentrated in the front line.

Most of the Highland contingents were on the right wing under the earls of Argyll and Lennox, and it seems that at this point they had still received no orders. Perhaps James had forgotten them, or conceivably, he was reluctant to rely on either their loyalty or their old-fashioned style of fighting; he may not have been aware that the similarly equipped Gordons had already been victorious on the opposite wing. The Highlanders were still hesitating when Sir Edward Stanley's detachment appeared on their flank. Its approach would have been hidden until the last moment below the rim of the hill on that side, allowing no time to deploy to meet it. Exactly what happened next is uncertain, but it appears that the clansmen, unable to form a solid defensive line before the English were upon them, threw themselves piecemeal at their assailants in a series of desperate charges. Here the lightness of their armour was a definite disadvantage, because Stanley's archers broke up their attacks at close range with heavy casualties, while his billmen and cavalry pushed forward onto the ridge. Eventually the Highlanders broke and fled; among those left dead on the field were both earls in command, alongside Lachlan MacLean, successor to Hector Odhar who commanded at Bloody Bay, and the chief of the Frasers of Lovat (Sadler & Serdiville, 2012). However, Iain MacIain and Iye Roy Mackay escaped, though the latter's brother, John Riabhach, the victor of Aldicharrish, was killed. John of Killin, chief of the Mackenzies, is listed among the casualties by Sadler and Serdiville but in fact survived, which supports the story related by Mackenzie (1894) that he was captured but later escaped. He lived to be captured again by the English at the Battle of Pinkie in 1547, and died in 1561. His uncle, Hector Roy, also escaped from Flodden, though most of their clansmen are said to have been killed.

In the short term, the consequences of the defeat for Scotland were catastrophic, although Bishop Leslie of Ross almost manages to make it seem like a Scottish victory. The casualty list included the king, the Lord High Treasurer, the Archbishop of St Andrews, the Bishop of the Isles, nine earls, fourteen other Lords of Parliament, about 300 lesser gentry and anything between 5,000 and 12,000 others (Sadler & Serdiville). Taking the lowest estimate, this might represent 1 per cent of the population of the country killed in a single afternoon. For comparison, the death rate for the United Kingdom in the four years of the First World War was roughly 2 per cent, but of course casualties are not spread out evenly in the course of a long war, and a better comparison might be with the single worst day for the British Army in the Great War, 1st July 1916, when nearly 20,000 men were killed. In proportion to the population, Scotland's losses on the day of Flodden were at least twenty times as high. Furthermore, they fell disproportionately on the ruling class, which must raise the question of how a society could survive such a blow without profound consequences for its economy and governance, not to mention the traumatising effect on the individual survivors and bereaved families. But it seems that the Highland clans escaped relatively lightly, though by how much is difficult to quantify. Certainly, there was no detectable pause in the squabbles in the north, and clans that had fought side by side at Flodden were soon once again at each others' throats. James's death left yet another infant on the throne, his son James V, while the government of Scotland came under the control of John Stewart, second duke of Albany, who was now second in line to the throne and took over as regent. Albany, however, was unpopular with the Scottish nobility and between 1517 and 1521, he spent most of his time in France, leaving the Highlanders to their own devices.

The field of Flodden, although well outside the Highlands, is well worth visiting for anyone with an interest in the military history of the clans. In stark contrast to the other fields discussed in this book, the site is well known and preserved, complete with a battlefield trail with useful interpretation boards. The site is a large one, but can be easily circumnavigated in a couple of hours. It is still open farmland, and a good overall impression can be had from one of several viewpoints. The drainage ditch that runs along the bottom of Branxton Hill marks the location of the mire in which the Scots were destroyed, but it is a modern feature, and in 1513 the boggy ground would have extended for some distance on either side of it (Younger, 2012). There is a car park (grid reference NT888373) about 400 yards west of the village of Branxton, from where a short but steep path leads up to the memorial. Branxton can be reached by a minor road off the A697 north of Wooler, Northumberland.

Chapter 9

'In an Hour of Need They Came': Torran Dubh

Date: 1517
Location: Near Rogart, Strath Fleet, Sutherland
Combatants: Mackays and allies versus Clans Sutherland, Ross, Murray, Gordon and Gunn
Outcome: Sutherland victory

The rivalry between the Mackays and the Sutherlands had continued intermittently after the former's victory at Druim na Coub, despite the Mackays' preoccupation with new enemies in Caithness and Easter Ross and the temporary alliance between the two houses at Aldicharrish. The immediate cause of the Torran Dubh campaign, however, was a civil war within the house of Sutherland. In 1514, the ninth Earl, John de Moravia, died childless and was succeeded by his sister Elizabeth, a woman 'full of spirit and witt' in the words of Sir Robert Gordon, who was married to Adam Gordon, son of the chief of Clan Gordon, Alexander, third earl of Huntly. Elizabeth's illegitimate younger brother, Alexander Sutherland of Kilphedder, also claimed the earldom, and a court was convened at Inverness to decide between them. Alexander failed to turn up, alleging that his life would be in danger if he did so, and the jury decided in favour of his sister. She and her husband were awarded all the Sutherland lands by a royal charter in June 1515, after which Adam Gordon took the title of earl of Sutherland, with his wife as countess. However, Alexander continued to press his claim, and in 1516 he captured the Sutherlands' seat at Dunrobin Castle while Adam was absent. The earl responded by making an agreement with John Sinclair, third earl of Caithness, by which each would support the other, but it seems that it was the earl of Huntly, in his capacity as Sheriff of Inverness-shire, who actually recovered Dunrobin and arrested Alexander for the offence of appropriating royal revenues. In any case, Alexander is known to have been in prison in Edinburgh between March 1517 and February of the following year (Fraser, 1892), which is significant because Sir Robert Gordon's claim that he was in command at Torran Dubh cannot therefore be correct.

According to Robert Mackay (1829), Earl John of Caithness attempted to honour his agreement with the Sutherlands by subverting another of their enemies, the Mackays, whose chief, John, had very recently succeeded his father, Iye Roy. The earl therefore backed the rival claim of John Mackay's uncle, Neil, and sent a force from Caithness to support Neil's two sons in an invasion of Strath Naver. But John's brother Donald defeated and killed them at Dail Naivigh near Loch Naver, whereupon Earl John handed Neil over to the Mackays to be executed and withdrew from the conflict. With one of the Sutherlands' most powerful allies thus neutralised, John Mackay unleashed his clansmen against Adam and Elizabeth. His motive for doing so at this time is not entirely clear. Robert Mackay says that he feared the expansion of the Gordons, who he believed intended to subdue the entire northern part of the kingdom, and had been actively seeking the support of other clans, including the Mackenzies, Mackintoshes and even the Mackays' old enemies the Rosses, in preventing this. The author of 'Conflicts of the Clans' thought that he simply wanted to capitalise on the ongoing civil strife in Sutherland 'to try if he could gain anything by spoiling that country', while Robert Gordon suggests that he wished to take advantage of the fact that Adam was absent in the south, leaving his wife in charge at Dunrobin. The same authority goes on to say that Elizabeth persuaded her brother Alexander to command the Sutherland forces, but as mentioned above, this must be an error. In fact, as Sir Robert himself admits that Alexander was on friendly terms with the Mackays and later married John's sister, it seems more probable that he had helped to incite the Mackay invasion rather than agreed to repel it.

Robert Mackay notes the battle that followed only briefly, and is clearly sceptical of Sir Robert Gordon's claim that the Mackays were defeated with very few losses on the Sutherland side. Angus Mackay (1906) concurs with his namesake's dismissal of the Sutherland historian, citing his statement that Alexander of Kilphedder was present as proof of the unreliability of his account, and has fun mocking other claims made by Gordon, who lists at least six disastrous defeats that were allegedly inflicted on the Mackays during this period, but which evidently failed to stop them returning to the fray and even advancing their cause. Nevertheless, Gordon appears to have been correct to state that the Mackays gathered a very large army from Strath Naver, Assynt and all the lands in the far north-west. There were also, apparently, contingents from the Mathesons of Sutherland and the Polsons, a Caithness family that was regarded as a sept or branch of Clan Mackay.

According to the account in 'Conflicts of the Clans', a Sutherland army led by John Moray intercepted John Mackay's eastward advance 'at a place called Torran Dubh' in Strath Fleet, 'where there ensued a fierce and cruel conflict'. In the initial clash the Mackay advance guard was 'chased' or driven in on the main body, whereupon John gathered a picked force of his best warriors and counterattacked, delegating his brother Donald to guard his rear. This source, apparently relying on Sir Robert Gordon, simply concludes that after further fierce fighting, 'well fought on either side', the Sutherland men were victorious. They later found 216 Strath Naver men dead on the field in addition to others killed in the pursuit, while Niall Macean-Macangus of Assynt and many of his men were also killed. The Sutherland army was said to have lost only thirty-eight of their own men. However, Angus Mackay (1906) has suggested that there may have been an additional explanation for the collapse of the formidable Mackays. He quotes a manuscript history of Clan Gunn that tells how a Gunn war party, arriving from the north, appeared unexpectedly on top of a ridge overlooking the battlefield while the fighting was still going on and the Mackays were gradually driving their opponents back. Whether they had set out to join the Sutherland coalition or whether their appearance was pure coincidence we are not told, but the Gunns had of course suffered heavily at the hands of the Mackays in previous campaigns, and they seized the opportunity to take their revenge. Charging down the hill into the unguarded flank of their enemies, they quickly turned the tide of the battle. Although we are not told so specifically, it is likely that an attack from this direction would have trapped the Mackays against the river Fleet and made it more difficult for them to extricate themselves. Angus Mackay quotes a poem of unknown date from the Gunn manuscript, which he translates as follows:

> The Gunns came, and came they did,
> T'was in an hour of need they came.
> The Mackays and the Mathesons fled,
> But the Polsons were mercilessly slain.

Despite its lack of corroboration from other sources, this account seems very plausible. The poem would hardly be remembered and passed down without having some basis in truth, while the Sutherland sources would have had an obvious reason for ignoring the contribution of the Gunns in order to magnify their own achievements. It does not explain why the Polsons suffered so severely, but we can assume that they were in an exposed position, which made it difficult for them to rally and fight their way out; possibly, they comprised part of the picked force led by John. It is also possible that the Gunns, who were their neighbours in Caithness, had particular reasons to dislike them. John Mackay himself survived, however, and soon afterwards, according to 'Conflicts of the Clans', sent his brothers Donald and William to renew the attack on the Sutherlands. But at a place called Loch Sallachie they encountered John Moray and were again defeated, with both Mackay brothers being killed along with Moray's brother John Roy of Aberscross. However, Angus Mackay (1906) denies that the clan was defeated, despite their losses, pointing out that the Mackays managed to burn the village of Pitfure near the site where the Battle of Torran Dubh was fought, and in 1518, they secured a title to lands in the parish of Rogart. In the same year, the Mackays signed a bond of friendship with Adam Gordon, which left the latter free to settle his account with Alexander of Kilphedder. Robert Mackay relates Alexander's subsequent fate in a tale reminiscent of Shakespeare. He had allegedly been told by some witches that his head was destined to be raised higher than any of the Sutherlands, and had chosen to interpret this as foretelling a glorious career. But although at some point after the Battle of Torran Dubh he again managed to seize Dunrobin Castle, Earl Adam soon returned and drove him out. He then resorted to ravaging the earl's lands along the east coast, but Adam sent his vassal, Alexander Leslie of Kinniuvy, to find the raiders and pin them until the earl's own army arrived. However, Leslie took them by surprise at a place called Alltachuilain near Loth, south of present-day Helmsdale, captured Alexander of Kilphedder and beheaded him on the spot. The prophecy was fulfilled when Alexander's severed head was placed on a spear, taken back to Dunrobin and displayed on the highest tower.

The most likely site for the Battle of Torran Dubh is on the level ground beside the river Fleet about a mile north-east of the village of Pittentrail (grid reference NC712037), which is about 9 miles east of Lairg on the A839. A good view can be obtained from the opposite side of the road near Pitfure Church (grid reference NC714036). The ridge behind the church is presumably the one over which the Gunns arrived. Three trains a day in each direction on the Inverness to Wick line stop at Rogart Station outside Pittentrail.

Chapter 10

The Fall of the House of MacIain: Creag an Airgid

Date: *c.*1519
Location: Near Kilchoan, Ardnamurchan
Combatants: MacIains of Ardnamurchan versus MacDonalds and MacLeods under Sir Donald MacDonald of Lochalsh
Outcome: MacDonald victory

Almost cut off from the rest of the mainland by sea lochs, Ardnamurchan has always been more accessible by sea than by land, and in many ways is best thought of as belonging to the Inner Hebrides rather than to the mainland. In the fifteenth century it was the stronghold of the MacIains, a branch of Clan Donald which traced its descent from Iain Sprangach ('The Bold') MacDonald, whose brother Angus Og had fought alongside Robert the Bruce at Bannockburn. The clan was also known as the MacDonalds of Ardnamurchan, but in view of the large number of different branches of Clan Donald already in this story, the name MacIain will be adopted here in order to avoid confusion. The MacIain stronghold, Mingary Castle near Kilchoan, had originally been built by the MacDougalls in the thirteenth century, but was probably forfeited as a result of that clan's opposition to the Bruces, and placed under the control of its new owners sometime in the later fourteenth century. The MacIain chiefs went on to enjoy a privileged position in the councils of the Lords of the Isles (see Chapter 5), but by the beginning of the sixteenth century this was all in the past. After the last Lord of the Isles forfeited his title in 1493, the military power of the separate branches of Clan Donald was by no means broken and several of the chiefs refused to accept the royal decree, but Iain, chief of the MacIains, made the fateful decision to support the king. James visited the Hebrides in person to ensure the allegiance of the remaining local chiefs, and a charter issued by him in October of that year shows that he was actually staying at Mingary at that time as Iain's guest (Gregory). Among the other MacDonald leaders, Alexander of Lochalsh and Sir John MacDonald of Islay, the grandson of Donald Balloch, both submitted to him and received in return royal charters for their lands, as did John MacLean of Lochbuie and Duncan Mackintosh, Captain of Clan Chattan. However, John of Islay was obliged to allow a royal garrison to be posted in Dunaverty Castle in his ancestral lands in Kintyre, an imposition that he found intolerable. So as soon as James sailed away from the castle, John stormed it from the landward side, captured the royal governor and hanged him from the battlements in full view of the king's departing ship (Gregory). James was naturally furious, but his fleet had already dispersed and so he was unable to respond immediately. He therefore charged Iain MacIain with arresting the traitor. In 1494, MacIain surprised John and four of his sons on Islay and handed them over to James, who had them all executed.

In 1495, James was back at Mingary with an army, receiving the submission of most of the Highland and Island chiefs and binding the MacDonalds and their allies in the sum of £500 to keep the peace amongst themselves. But two years later, Alexander of Lochalsh once again attacked the Mackenzies – perhaps, as Gregory suggests, in an attempt to obtain revenge for his defeat at Blar na Parc. He was defeated at the Battle of Drumchatt and returned to the southern Hebrides in the hope of raising a fresh army, but he was assassinated on the island of Oronsay by an agent of Iain MacIain. By these actions, MacIain secured the favour of the king, but also earned the undying hatred of his MacDonald neighbours. While James IV lived he was able to deter any attempt at vengeance, and in 1505, he issued a further charter confirming MacIain in his possession of Ardnamurchan and the castle at Mingary. But James's death at Flodden eight years later left a power vacuum of which the MacDonalds were quick to take advantage. Alexander's son, Sir Donald of Lochalsh, who had apparently been knighted on the battlefield of Flodden for his zeal in fighting for the late king, proclaimed himself Lord of the Isles towards the end of 1513. The regent, Albany, lacked James IV's energy and revived the old practice of controlling the Highlands by appointing local magnates as his lieutenants. He charged Colin, third earl of Argyll, to keep the peace in the Isles, but by this time Sir Donald of Lochalsh had become a formidable power in his own right, putting together an alliance including the MacLeans of Duart, the MacLeods of the Lewis, Harris and Raasay branches, and Alexander MacDonald of Islay, another son of the executed John, who despite being related to the MacIains by marriage had thrown in his lot with the faction that offered to avenge his father's death.

In 1516, Sir Donald came to an agreement with Argyll that seems to have left him with his power base intact, and in either that or the following year he and Alexander of Islay landed in Ardnamurchan, ravaged MacIain's lands and temporarily occupied Mingary Castle. According to Gregory's account, the Royal Council ordered him to return the castle to its rightful owner, but he refused and instead razed it to the ground, though in fact it appears to have suffered little damage. Gregory says that Sir Donald was only forced to retreat by a mutiny among his followers, who feared the consequences of his reckless defiance of the Council. But either two or three years later – the date of the battle of Creag an Airgid is variously given as 1518 or 1519 – they returned to finish the business. Donald gathered a fleet on Skye, which comprised contingents from most of his allies in the northern Hebrides – the MacDonalds of Lochalsh and their allies the MacLeods of Lewis and Raasay – and led it south to rendezvous with Alexander of Islay.

For a long time the location of the battle that followed seems to have been lost. Donald Gregory, like most early commentators, places it on the Morvern Peninsula, Ardnamurchan's counterpart on the southern side of Loch Sunart, and it was not until the early twentieth century that it became evident that the inhabitants of Ardnamurchan had preserved a tradition that could locate it more precisely. The first attempt to identify the site seems to have been made by Angus Henderson, who in his 'Ardnamurchan Place Names' (1915) mentions a knoll where 'tradition says' that the three MacIain leaders who died there were buried 'close under the south-west side of Creag an Airgid and near the old march [the boundary] between the farms of Kilchoan and Glendrian'. The rank and file, says Henderson, were interred a short distance to the south, 'at a place which can also be pointed out'. Unfortunately, subsequent researchers have been unable to locate the exact spot referred to, although M.E.M. Donaldson (1926) mentioned some cairns in a hollow on the right side of the road from Kilchoan to Sanna. Creag an Airgid is a hill in the interior of the Ardnamurchan Peninsula, approximately 3 miles north of Mingary Castle on the south coast. The name means 'Silver Crag', though its origin is uncertain. The hill is in no way distinctive in colour, and there are no silver deposits in the region. Jon Haylett (on clanMacIain.com – *see* Sources and Further Reading) suggests that it may have been a place where cattle drovers were paid ('*airgid*' means money as well as silver in Gaelic). For our purposes, its significance is that it overlooks the most direct route to Mingary from Sanna Bay on the north side of the peninsula. Sanna has a sandy beach on which galleys could be drawn up out of the water for safety and is protected by a sandy reef offshore, making it the most likely landing place for a seaborne invader coming from the north who wished to avoid the perilous voyage around Ardnamurchan Point. This makes much more sense from a strategic point of view than the theory that an invader coming from the direction of Skye and presumably aiming for the heartland of the lords of Ardnamurchan was brought to battle in Morvern, several miles to the south. It was therefore probably here that Sir Donald joined up with Alexander of Islay, whom Gregory says was present at the ensuing battle. It may seem strange that the burial cairns have now been lost, but the whole area is littered with natural boulders and heaps of stones of various sizes, remnants of the hard volcanic rocks eroded by glaciers during the Ice Ages, and once an artificial cairn had begun to collapse or be worn down, over time it would become difficult to distinguish it from these natural features. Consequently, it seems now to be impossible without extensive excavation to establish which of these rock piles, if any, mark the battlefield and its graves. In 2014, Jon Haylett noted a conspicuous stone on the side of the road, the flat top of which was covered with smaller stones that had been deliberately placed there over many years. He speculated that the tradition might have originated because the stone had once commemorated those slain in the battle, or alternatively that it was a convenient spot to distribute money to the cattle drovers. It is, however, clearly a natural object in situ, so even if it is related to the battle, the stone is of limited value for locating the exact site.

The battlefield itself is particularly interesting because of its location on the rim of a giant volcanic crater, of which Creag an Airgid itself forms a part. The original volcano was formed about 60 million years ago, and during the Ice Ages it was ground down by the glaciers to leave the present-day feature, which comprises a roughly circular area of flat boggy ground about 2 miles across, surrounded by a ring of low rocky hills, the remains of the hard volcanic rocks that managed to resist the glacial erosion. The crater is very obvious in satellite photographs and on the OS 1:25000 map, but it is less so on the ground, partly because of its sheer size, and it is unlikely that any of the participants in the battle would have realised that they were inside a crater. Nevertheless, the steep rocky slopes of the rim and the extensive bogs on the lower ground must have seriously restricted the space available to deploy even a small clan army. If we discount the idea that men were drawn up on the steep rocky slopes of the hill itself and charged down them into battle, the most likely spot for the MacIains to have deployed to meet invaders coming from Sanna is about 600 metres north-north west of Creag an Airgid, where the modern Sanna road crosses a stream known as the Allt Uamha na Muice (the Stream of the Sow's Cave). Here a low ridge of slightly drier ground overlooking the ford from the west would allow a defending force to threaten the flank of an enemy as he advanced over another slightly higher ridge on the far side of the stream, the Druim Liath, or Grey Ridge, and then struggled across the ford. At the crossing point, where they would inevitably bunch together as they waited their turn to get over the stream, Sir Donald's men would also have been at the optimum range for MacIain archers to target them with arrows.

But despite all their precautions, the MacIains were unable to defeat the invaders. We know nothing of the actual course of the fighting except that MacIain and his two sons, John of Sunart and Angus, were all killed. This high rate of casualties among the leaders suggests that the defenders might have been outflanked or encircled, rather than simply pushed back and forced to flee. The exact date of the encounter is as difficult to establish as its location, but Donald Gregory quotes Privy Seal documents to the effect that John MacIain was dead by 18 August 1519. If Mingary Castle was in fact Sir Donald's objective, it seems that he did not succeed in recapturing it, because he died suddenly very soon after the battle (Gregory). Both Hugh MacDonald and Niall MacMhuirich's 'Red Book of Clanranald' record his death, but the cause is not given and the two sources disagree about the location. Evidently, he had been taken to an offshore island, said to have been either Mull or Tiree, but in view of the timing, it is highly likely that he died of wounds sustained in the fight at Creag an Airgid.

When news of the battle reached the earl of Argyll, he was furious that his previous leniency towards the rebellious MacDonalds had been exploited in this fashion, and attempted to push through Parliament a sentence of forfeiture against Sir Donald which had been commenced on account of a previous charge of treason. At this point, he was presumably unaware that the accused was already dead. However, he met with opposition among those who either sympathised with the Islemen or feared the expansion of Argyll's own power, and Gregory records the solemn protest he made before Parliament, disclaiming all responsibility for the turmoil in the Highlands unless his advice was listened to and he was given the men and supplies he had been promised. In this atmosphere, Sir Donald of Lochalsh might once again have escaped retribution after the killing of MacIain had he survived, but as it happened, his allies quickly dispersed and the rebellion was soon over. He left no heir, which meant that the only MacDonald leader who was prominent enough to act as a focus for those who remained loyal to the idea of the lordship was Donald Dubh, the son of Angus Og, who was still in prison. It would be ironic if, despite the crushing defeat that the house of MacIain had suffered, it was an anonymous warrior of that clan who had put an end to the latest attempt to restore the Lords of the Isles.

Even today, Ardnamurchan is difficult to access by land. The most direct route is via the A82 south from Fort William and the ferry crossing across Loch Linnhe at Corran, then the A861 to Salen. From there the mostly single track B8007 leads to the village of Kilchoan. There is a bus service on this route once a day in each direction, but the return trip requires an overnight stay at Kilchoan. Alternatively, the village can be reached by a frequent ferry service from Tobermory on Mull, which in turn is accessible by ferry from Oban. About a mile north of the centre of Kilchoan, a minor road branches off to Sanna Bay; follow the signs to the lighthouse in Kilchoan village and then take the first turning on the right towards Sanna. Creag an Airgid hill (grid reference NM476668) is on the right of this road, about 3 miles north of Kilchoan. The grid reference of the ridge overlooking the Allt Uamha na Muice is NM474673. Mingary Castle (grid reference NM502631) is situated on the shore about a mile and a half east of Kilchoan. It is now a hotel and is not open to casual visitors, so is best viewed from the Tobermory ferry.

Chapter 11

'More Like Lyons than Men': Blar na Leine

Date: 15 July 1544
Location: Laggan Locks, Loch Lochy
Combatants: MacDonalds of Clanranald versus Clan Fraser of Lovat
Outcome: Clanranald victory

The latest phase of minority government in Scotland came to an end in 1528, when the 16-year-old James V escaped from his guardians and took over the reins of power. James was an energetic ruler whose reign seemed to promise a great deal, but he inherited a country still threatened by its English neighbour and increasingly riven by religious conflict as the ideas of the Protestant Reformation spread. According to the traditional account, it was some two years before the Battle of Creag an Airgid that Martin Luther nailed his Ninety-five Theses criticising the practices of the Roman Catholic Church to the door of a church in Wittenberg, Germany. The new ideas quickly spread, and in the same year as James seized power the first Scottish Protestant martyr, Patrick Hamilton, was burned at the stake for heresy. The king remained a staunch supporter of the Catholic Church, and resisted calls from Henry VIII to follow his lead in abolishing the monasteries, but he did his best to maintain peace with England and did not initiate a large-scale persecution. He was considered to be sympathetic to the common people, and consequently, one of his key policies was to curb the power of the nobility, especially in peripheral and traditionally lawless regions like the Borders and the

Highlands. The latter had in fact descended further than ever into anarchy since the suppression of the lordship of the Isles, leading to the multi-sided bloodbath known as the *Linn nan Creach* or 'Age of Raids', in which the clans settled old scores and contended for power without fear of intervention by either the defunct Lords of the Isles or the weak and distracted central government.

Sir Donald of Lochalsh was dead, and Donald Dubh, whom many in the Hebrides still regarded as the legitimate successor to the lordship, had been in prison ever since his capture in 1506. But eventually, the resulting power vacuum led to the rise of yet another claimant, Donald Gorm MacDonald of Sleat. In 1539, in alliance with the MacLeods of Lewis, this Donald ravaged his family's old rivals the MacLeods of Trotternish on Skye, then, taking advantage of the absence of the chief of the Mackenzies, crossed to the mainland and attacked the latter's castle at Eilean Donan. The place was held only by a handful of men and its capture seemed unavoidable; J. Mackay (1924) says that the only occupants were the constable, Duncan MacRae, and two other men, and that they had only one bow and one arrow between them. However, Donald rashly exposed himself within bow shot of the walls while supervising the assault, and Duncan shot him in the knee with his arrow. In a rage, Donald pulled out the arrowhead, but one of the barbs cut an artery. He was taken to a nearby island, where he bled to death within sight of his objective. His shocked and demoralised men burned all the Mackenzies' boats by way of revenge and returned to Skye.

Despite this ignominious end to Donald Gorm's brief rebellion, it was enough to convince King James that there was still work to do in pacifying the Isles. So, in May 1540, the king undertook a major naval expedition to Orkney and the Hebrides, with twelve ships equipped with heavy artillery and packed with soldiers. Previous royal expeditions to the west coast had been hindered by the difficulty of finding safe routes for large sailing vessels through the maze of lochs and islands, but this time an expert navigator, Alexander Lindsay, was employed to chart the course. No Highland chief possessed any means of countering the ships' guns, and no resistance was offered. Nevertheless, the king adopted the cautious if dishonourable practice introduced by James I, of holding courts at various places to investigate alleged crimes, if necessary luring his victims with offers of negotiation, and then arresting them. From Orkney the fleet sailed west to Lewis and then Skye, where the MacLeod chiefs of Lewis and Dunvegan were taken into custody, after which James arrived in Trotternish, the scene of Donald Gorm's depredations. Among those placed under arrest there was Iain Moidertach, or Iain of Moidart, Captain of the MacDonalds of Clanranald. Iain was an illegitimate son of the previous chief, Alexander, and appears to have succeeded him because of his popularity with the influential families of the clan. Charles MacDonald (1889) describes him as 'unquestionably the ablest as well as the most intrepid of all those who at any period ruled the clan'. He had been in possession of Castle Tioram, the Clanranald stronghold near Acharacle in Ardnamurchan, since around 1530, and was a close ally of the surviving McIains of the area. MacDonald remarks that there is no record of him being involved in any rebellion or disturbance in the following decade, and that in fact he had personally given his allegiance to the king, so that his arrest was 'worse than a political blunder, it was a downright breach of trust'. However, there must be a suspicion that Iain had committed some offence, since while most of the captured chiefs were quickly released in exchange for hostages or pledges of allegiance, Iain was not among them. Instead he was taken back to Edinburgh with the fleet and imprisoned there, while his clan was placed under the command of a rival claimant, Ranald, nicknamed Gallda, or 'the foreigner', who had the support of the Frasers of Lovat, since his mother was a Fraser and he had been fostered by that clan as a youth.

But scarcely more than two years later, at the age of only 30, James V was dead. War had finally broken out with England in October 1542, and in November, the Scots suffered a serious defeat at the hands of a numerically inferior force of English border horsemen at Solway Moss. The king died in the following month, allegedly from despair at the humiliation, but more likely from a recurring infection, since he had been ill on several occasions previously. His only surviving heir, Mary, later known as Queen of Scots, was six days old. Despite opposition from a Catholic faction led by Cardinal Beaton, who plausibly claimed that James had appointed him as regent, it was the Protestant James Hamilton, earl of Arran, who actually took control. Arran pursued a pro-English policy at first, and in 1543 signed the Treaty of Greenwich, according to which Mary was to be married to Henry VIII's son, Edward. The Catholic faction, however, remained a threat, gaining the support of the powerful earls of Lennox, Argyll and Huntly, and in a desperate attempt to counter them, Arran released from prison the remainder of the clan chiefs whom James V had arrested three years earlier. Among these was Iain Moidertach. Ranald Gallda had proved unpopular with the Clanranalds, in part because of his frugality, which was regarded by those clansmen who traditionally enjoyed the favour of the chiefs as bordering on meanness; he became known as 'Ranald of the Chickens', because he had proposed to substitute poultry for beef at his inauguration feast. So, when Iain returned to Castle Tioram, the clan welcomed him at once, and Ranald fled to take refuge with his kinsmen, the Frasers of Lovat. These were a branch of the Lowland family of Fraser, which was originally from France and had gained royal favour for the service of Sir Simon Fraser, who fought at Bannockburn. By 1367, one of his descendants, Hugh, was being styled 'Lord of Lovat and the Aird', both of which were districts on the southern side of the Beauly Firth, near Inverness, which he had probably acquired by marriage (Fraser, 1952). From then on, the Frasers of Lovat gradually extended their possessions and adopted the role of Highland chiefs. By the middle of the fifteenth century, their lands extended as far as Strath Errick above the eastern shore of Loch Ness. They remained loyal supporters of the monarchy, and sometime around 1460, their chief, another Hugh, was created Lord Fraser of Lovat. To their Gaelic-speaking tenants and neighbours, however, the heads of the family were always known as 'MacShimi', or son of Simon.

Knowing that retribution would soon follow, Iain Moidertach set about raising an army. He was joined by other disaffected branches of the MacDonald family, including those of Glengarry and Keppoch, as well as the MacIains from Ardnamurchan and the Camerons from Lochaber. Early in the summer of 1544, the allies swept along the Great Glen in a pre-emptive attack on the Fraser lands, in the course of which they ravaged Strath Errick and temporarily captured the famous stronghold of Urquhart Castle on Loch Ness, then held by the Laird of Grant, an ally of the Frasers. The task of restoring order fell to George Gordon, the fourth earl of Huntly, the grandson of the third earl who had fought at Flodden, and an experienced soldier who had recently defeated an English army at the Battle of Haddon Rig (1542). Huntly raised a royal army from the districts around Aberdeen and led it into Lochaber, where he was joined by Hugh Fraser, third Lord Lovat, and his clansmen, as well as contingent of Grants and the lone figure of Ranald Gallda, hopeful of being restored to his position. The Clanranalds avoided battle by retreating into the Rough Bounds of Moidart, but Huntly decided not to pursue further than Inverlochy on Loch Linnhe. He proclaimed a victory, announced that Ranald was restored to the chieftainship of Clan Ranald, and marched home to Aberdeenshire, taking the most direct route up Glen Spean towards Strathspey and Badenoch.

However, when the army reached the head of Glen Spean, which connects with the southern end of Loch Lochy about 5 miles north of the present site of Fort William, Lord Lovat decided to leave the main body and return to his own lands by a shorter route, continuing north-east up the Great Glen towards Loch Ness and Strath Errick. All our sources agree that Huntly advised him against this, since the small force of no more than 400 Frasers would be very vulnerable if it were to be intercepted. But according to James Fraser's seventeenth-century 'Polychronicon', or 'Fraser Chronicle' (Fraser, 1905), which is one of our main sources for the subsequent events, Lovat remained adamant. One of his relatives, James Fraser of Foynes, who is described by the 'Fraser Chronicle' as a 'headstrong man', was especially vocal in arguing that the clan should go it alone. He believed that this number of the clan's warriors would be a match for any hostile force they might encounter, while if they took a longer route home under the protection of their allies, they might be accused of cowardice. Ranald Gallda, who clearly had no confidence in Huntly's advertised victory and had elected to return with the royal army rather than try to return to Moidart, remained with his Fraser relatives when the force divided.

Clanranald scouts had in fact been keeping the army under observation throughout the campaign, and as soon as it became divided, Iain Moidertach set out to cut off the Frasers, who were both the weakest of the two forces and the most immediately threatening. Lord Lovat's men had gone only another 5 or 6 miles beyond Glen Spean and were marching along the southern shore of Loch Lochy, along the route followed by the modern A82, when they became aware that they were being shadowed by a larger force of Clanranalds on the far side of the loch. Iain Moidertach's army was marching along the lower slopes of Ben Tee with banners flying, from which it could be deduced that they were organised into seven companies, including contingents from the MacDonalds of Moidart, Knoydart, Morar and Ardnamurchan as well as from their allies the Camerons. They were travelling light and were making such good progress that Lovat quickly realised that they would intercept him at the northern end of the loch. James Fraser adds that he detached a part of his force, a hundred archers under a man named Bean Clerach (more plausibly rendered by Mackay (1905) as Iain Cleirich), to occupy 'a pass in the hills at a little distance' in order to secure his retreat if he should be defeated. The location of this pass is not specified, but it would presumably have been somewhere on the south-eastern side of the glen, since he would hardly have planned to retreat westwards, towards the country of the Clanranalds. Fraser says that Cleirich accidentally went 'beyond Drumglach' so that he was unable to assist his comrades, and the pass that he should have held was occupied by the enemy. Drumglach is probably the height marked on the early OS maps as Druim Glaoidh ('Sticky Ridge'), overlooking Letter Finlay (Cowan, 2017), but as this is well away from the lochside and about 3 miles south of the battlefield, it is difficult to see how such a mistake could have been made. It is of course possible that Cleirich's action was not an accident at all, but a deliberate act of either cowardice or treachery. Lovat was now left with around 300 men – mostly Frasers, with a few Grants and Mackintoshes – compared to the 500 of his enemies, but the Frasers included many 'gentlemen' who would have been well equipped and armoured, whereas the Clanranalds were mostly 'of the inferior sort', or presumably more lightly equipped '*caterans*'. The Fraser chief was well known for having insisted that his followers were thoroughly trained in swordsmanship and archery (Cowan, 2017). He may therefore have entered the fight with a high degree of confidence, but James Fraser reports that just as the battle began, he was greatly distressed to be joined by his son, the Master of Lovat, whom he had ordered to remain at home, but who had been taunted by his stepmother for doing so while the older men were in peril. The implication of this is obviously that Lovat wished to avoid losing two generations of his family, and that he was already prepared for a particularly desperate fight.

It was said (perhaps first by James Fraser, writing in the 1660s) that the day was so hot that the warriors threw off their armour and fought in their shirts, hence the name by which the encounter was to become known – *Blar na Leine*, 'the Field (or Battle) of the Shirts'. However, the authors of the entry on the Canmore website prefer a derivation from *Blar na Leana*, 'the Field of the Swampy Meadow'. Certainly, the flat ground at the head of the loch is wet and boggy, and equally certainly not everyone discarded their armour, while many of those who did so, or perhaps never possessed it in the first place, were at a serious disadvantage. The 'Fraser Chronicle' tells us that although many men did fight in their shirts, 'running at each other like mastiffs' and even wrestling with each other in the waters of the loch, 'Such as bore armour, head pieces and coats of mail, knocked down their opponents without resistance like tender twigs of shrubs' (Fraser, 1905). But all agree that the fight was waged with greater than ordinary ferocity. Lovat's men, cornered with their backs to the loch, fought with the courage of desperation, while the Clanranalds had seen their country ravaged and their homes burned by the invaders, and were no doubt eager for revenge. Bishop Leslie's account says that the fight began with an exchange of arrows from a distance, 'which lasted a long time', until both sides had used up all their arrows. This was certainly the usual practice, but James Fraser does not mention this and implies that the two sides clashed hand to hand from the start, so if there was an initial archery duel it must actually have been of fairly short duration and resulted in few casualties. The Fraser account goes on to tell how they 'fought more like lyons than men with slashes and strokes, their arms two handed swords and Dence [i.e. Danish] axes, front to front… so fierce and forward that they seemed to fell one another like trees falling in a wood'. Even men who had been knocked down and left for dead would seize a dropped sword and hack at the legs of any enemies who came near them.

Local tradition preserved the details of several notable combats in this desperate mêlée. According to Charles MacDonald (1889), Ranald Gallda, who must have known that he could expect no mercy, fought with notable courage. He cut down one opponent after another until he came face to face with a man from Strontian remembered only by his patronymic, Mac Dhonuill Ruaidh, 'the son of Red Donald'. As Ranald approached him, Mac Dhonuill resorted to a stratagem, shouting out to his opponent to beware of an attacker behind him. Ranald apparently fell for this old trick and turned around, whereupon Mac Dhonuill ran forward and stabbed him fatally. But with his dying breath, Ranald dealt a back stroke with his sword, which struck his enemy on the head and inflicted a deep cut. The story went that Mac Dhonuill Ruaidh was carried home to Strontian, where the local doctor was bribed by some of the villagers to kill him by opening his skull wound even further. Their motive is unclear, but MacDonald states that 'some say' that the Strontian people were supporters of Ranald Gallda's claim to be the legitimate chief of Clanranald, while others argue that Mac Dhonuill had offended their sense of fair play by boasting about the killing of Ranald, even though it was well known that he had done so by a dishonourable trick. His skull, still showing the wound inflicted by his enemy's blade, was later exhumed and exhibited as a curiosity. Charles MacDonald reports that there was an old man still living when he wrote in the 1880s who had seen the skull and heard the story told in its presence. Another story tells of two champions, one a MacDonald and the other a Fraser, who accompanied their single combat with taunts delivered with a sort of gallows humour. The former struck the first blow with the words: 'Take that from Clanranald's blacksmith!' and the other riposted with 'And you receive this from MacShimie's blacksmith!' After the battle it was said that the bodies of these two men had been found lying side by side, having battered each other to death in this jocular fashion. The implication of such tales, if there is any truth in any of them, is that not only did some men at least square off for man-to-man duels, but that their neighbours might stop fighting to watch them, or at least that they were witnessed by survivors who would recall them later.

Gregory (1836) says that eventually, the Frasers' losses were so great that they contemplated retreat, presumably to the eastward away from the loch, but instead of the expected support of Iain Cleirich's detachment, they found the route blocked by yet more hostile MacDonalds. They therefore returned to the fray and fought until they were almost annihilated. Lovat himself was in the forefront, incensed by the death of his son who had fallen earlier in the fight, and distinguishing himself by the ferocious blows that he rained on his opponents. The Clanranalds may not have recognised him in his armour, but they nicknamed him Cruoy Choskir (probably 'Cniaidh Chasgair', the 'Hard Slayer'), and when he eventually fell they encouraged their comrades with joyful shouts of '*Huit Cruoy Choskir!*', 'The Hard Slayer has fallen!' When the fighting was finally over, amid what even the Clanranalds remembered as a 'shocking scene of slaughter' (MacDonald, 1889), they found the bodies of Lord Lovat, his son, three of his brothers, Ranald Gallda and nearly 300 of the Frasers. Gregory cites a letter from Donald Dubh to the English Privy Council, which gave a figure of thirteen score, or 260, of the ordinary warriors. This, however, may not be a complete tally since Bishop Leslie implies that 'a great number of commons' were killed in addition to the 300. As Cowan (2017) suggests, these might have been non-combatants, for example servants and porters, or just men too poorly armed to be counted as front-line fighters. The bodies were left on the field to be collected a few days later by their families and buried at Beauly Priory; the fact that they could have done so unmolested was rather unconvincingly cited by James Fraser as proof that his clan 'had the mastery' despite the slaughter. His namesake, James Fraser of Foynes, who had encouraged Lovat to split his forces and fight alone, was the only 'gentleman' captured alive, though he was badly wounded and according to one account died a few days later. Just four other Frasers escaped from the field. Clan Fraser sources later made extravagant claims for the losses they had inflicted on the enemy, alleging that only eight of the Clanranalds remained alive. But although many of them must certainly have fallen, especially in view of their apparent shortage of armour, they lost none of their leaders and were able to take the field again in the following year, which suggests that their casualties must have been far fewer than those of the vanquished.

Soon after the battle, the Scottish Parliament learned of the slaughter of the Frasers and summoned Iain Moidertach to face trial for treason, but he ignored the summons, and in the following year, he went onto the offensive. During the course of the 'Great Raid' of 1545, as it came to be known, the Clanranalds and Camerons once again captured Urquhart Castle. They seem to have met little opposition, and they looted the place thoroughly before retiring with 2,000 cattle and a wealth of other plunder, including the cannon, furniture and even bed linen. Urquhart was an unusually large and strong castle, and how a clan army without artillery or siege equipment could achieve this feat is not clear, though in fact this was the third time in three decades that the MacDonalds had seized it, the first being in the aftermath of the disaster at Flodden. Reid and Turner (2006) note that in 1527, Hector Boece had described the walls as 'ruinous', and suggest that the circuit was simply too big to be defended by a small garrison. Iain, along with other chiefs including the MacLeans and MacIains, then entered into negotiations with Henry VIII of England in what Charles MacDonald calls 'some nefarious plot against the Scots government'. It was for this, rather than for the fight at Blar na Leine, or the Great Raid, that he was outlawed and Huntly sent back to apprehend him with the aid of a contingent under William, chief of Clan Macintosh, who were longstanding enemies of the Camerons. Once again, Huntly did not dare to penetrate into Moidart, but he captured the chiefs of the Camerons and the MacDonalds of Keppoch, who were hanged at Elgin. Charles MacDonald says that this gave rise to a feud between the Keppochs and the Macintoshes, which lasted until 1688, when the former and their Cameron and Glengarry allies were victorious at the Battle of Mulroy in Lochaber. According to MacDonald, this was the last inter-clan battle fought in Scotland – a claim that, however, is made for several other encounters around the same time.

Huntly subsequently repaid William Macintosh for his help by arresting and executing him for an alleged plot against the earl, though it is likely that the underlying reason was the Catholic Huntly's dislike of the chief's support for the Protestant reformation. By this time, Scotland was once more at war with Henry VIII of England, who had been angered by Cardinal Beaton's refusal to countenance the marriage of Queen Mary to Henry's Protestant son. In 1546, Beaton was murdered by Protestant sympathisers, possibly in the pay of Henry, and in the following year an English army invaded Scotland, defeated the Scots at the Battle of Pinkie and occupied large parts of the south of the country in a campaign that came to be known as the 'Rough Wooing'. The 5-year-old Queen Mary was sent to France, where at the age of 16 she married King Francis III and briefly became queen of both countries. Back at home in 1548, the distracted Scottish government granted Iain Moidertach a pardon, but this seems to have been merely a temporary expedient, since four years later he was summoned to meet the earl of Arran at Aberdeen, and outlawed again when he prudently refused. In 1554, Queen Mary's mother, Mary of

Guise, took over the regency and a two-pronged attack was sent against the Clanranalds, with the earl of Argyll taking a fleet to attack Castle Tioram while Huntly advanced by land, but once again the plan failed. After Huntly's betrayal of William Macintosh, none of the clans was prepared to support him again, and his Lowland contingents, most of whom were cavalry, refused to risk their horses and themselves in the difficult terrain of Moidart. Meanwhile, Argyll had apparently landed artillery on the shore in order to bombard Castle Tioram, but the arrival of the Clanranald army forced him to withdraw it and he sailed his fleet away to deal with less intractable rebels in Skye and Harris. For some reason, Iain was now induced to accept a safe conduct from Arran, and he and two of his sons appeared in Edinburgh before Mary of Guise, whereupon they were arrested. They somehow escaped from prison and returned to Moidart, only to be outlawed yet again. Queen Mary returned to Scotland from France in 1561 after the death of her husband, Francis, and Iain's old adversary the earl of Huntly led an unsuccessful revolt against her, suspecting her of favouring the growing Protestant faction at court. Huntly died in captivity and was convicted of treason post-mortem. Five years after that, however, Iain Moidertach was not only still at large but still defiant, as the Lords of Parliament were requested to consider measures by which he could be '*dantonit*', or daunted (Gregory). It seems that they never did come up with any ideas, because Iain died peacefully at Castle Tioram in 1584, having ruled his clan, by Charles MacDonald's calculation, for fifty-four years.

Unlike most of the sites discussed in this book, the site of Blar na Leine is registered in the official Scottish Inventory of Historic Battlefields. The Highland Historic Environment Record identifies the area of the battle as extending along the eastern side of the Caledonian Canal from Laggan Locks where it enters Loch Lochy, approximately half a mile north-east to the settlement of South Laggan (grid reference NN287963). Like Blar na Parc, it has been subject to a metal detecting survey, but without result. Unfortunately, although the site is well known, it is not easy to envisage its appearance at the time of the battle. The Caledonian Canal was dug through the area in the 1820s, and according to Thomas Telford, the engineer in charge of the project, the level of Loch Lochy was raised by 12 feet in the process ('The Life of Thomas Telford, Civil Engineer, Written by Himself', in *The London Quarterly Review*, volume 63, 1839). This of course suggests that much of the ground where the fighting took place is now submerged.

Chapter 12

The 'Wild Scots' Subdued

The defeat at Blar na Leine did not finish the Frasers; the 'Fraser Chronicle' tells us that among the widows of the men who died were eighty who were pregnant with sons, all of whom grew to adulthood to replenish the fighting strength of the clan. In 1576, the funeral of the fifth Lord Lovat saw the mustering of a respectable total of between 800 and 900 clansmen, but they took further heavy losses in the civil wars of the following century. On the death of Elizabeth I of England in 1603, James VI of Scotland, the son of Mary Queen of Scots, became king of both countries, bringing to an end over 300 years of destructive rivalry between them, but this did not lead to a lasting peace. James's successor, Charles I, alienated both the English and Scottish parliaments and many of their people in quarrels over religion and taxation; by this time the majority of Scots, at least in the Lowlands, had adopted the form of Protestantism known as Presbyterianism, which rejected the rule of bishops and many aspects of the doctrine of the Church of England that Charles was keen to promote. These disputes led to the Bishops' Wars of 1639 and 1640 in Scotland, and eventually contributed to the outbreak of civil war in England in 1642. The Scots were brought into the conflict again in the following year with the signing of the Solemn League and Covenant, according to which the Church of Scotland and the English parliament agreed to resist Charles's religious reforms.

The chiefs of the Frasers of Lovat navigated these difficult waters with mixed results. In 1645, they unwisely took the side of the supporters of the Solemn League, known as the Covenanters, against the royalists led by the marquis of Montrose, and were beaten at the Battle of Auldearn. After the execution of Charles I in 1649, they followed the lead of the

Scottish Church and fought for the restoration of his son, Charles II, but were beaten again by Oliver Cromwell at Worcester in 1651. During the Jacobite rebellions of the eighteenth century, their allegiance was similarly vacillating. In the rising of 1745, the eleventh Lord Lovat, Simon Fraser, alienated both factions by his double-dealing before finally deciding for the losing side. His clansmen suffered heavy losses at Culloden, and Simon himself was taken to London and beheaded as a traitor, King George having commuted the normal sentence of hanging, drawing and quartering. He achieved posthumous fame as the last person in Britain to be executed by this method.

Few of the other clans featured in this story fared much better in the long run. The centralising tendency of central government, strengthened by gradually improving finances and communications as well as by technical advances in artillery, which made the old strongholds of the Highlands ever more vulnerable, was becoming irresistible. The subsequent fate of the various branches of Clan Donald merits a book in itself. With the disappearance of the latest claimant to the lordship of the Isles on the death of Donald Gorm, they began to feud amongst themselves, as well as with longstanding enemies like the Mackenzies and old allies like the MacLeans. In 1543, Donald Dubh once again escaped from prison and proclaimed himself Lord of the Isles in a last desperate attempt to revive his family's fortunes. He was joined by the MacDonalds of Islay, with whose help he ravaged Argyll, but he received limited support elsewhere. He still aspired to the sort of independent role that his ancestors had enjoyed a century earlier, and reached an agreement with Henry VIII of England, who hoped to use him as a distraction against the Scottish government. With the help of large amounts of English gold, Donald managed to gather a total of about 8,000 troops (Gregory, 1836). Half of these followed him to Ireland to support the English there, but he died suddenly, apparently of a fever, at Drogheda in 1545. Donald left only one illegitimate son, and any hope of reviving the independent lordship died with him. His followers could no longer even afford an appropriate funeral for him, and it was eventually paid for by Henry VIII.

During the later sixteenth century, the reformation and consequent religious differences exacerbated the divisions in the Highlands. By the time Queen Mary returned in 1561, the Protestant faction was dominant, and it remained so in the Lowlands and at court despite the queen's own adherence to the Catholic faith, but most of the MacDonalds as well as many other Highland clans remained Catholic. The MacDonalds of Dunyvaig came closest to inheriting the mantle of the old Lords of the Isles, but in the early seventeenth century their old rival Archibald Campbell, the seventh earl of Argyll, manoeuvred their chiefs into a hopeless rebellion. The details of the legal disputes involved are complex (see Gregory, 1836, and Fraser-Mackintosh, 1895), but Grant (1952) succinctly identifies the Campbells as 'agents provocateurs, court wire-pullers, judges, executioners and recipients of the swag'. After the rebellion of Donald Gorm, the island of Islay had been given to the MacLeans by King James V, and although it was later restored, the hostilities between the two clans, which the government had deliberately provoked, continued. The MacLeans were finally defeated at the Battle of Ceann Traigh Ghruinneart in 1598, but Argyll continued to portray the MacDonalds at court as rebels. After 1603, James VI was determined to bring both his kingdoms under centralised control, all the more so as he had been brought up to regard the Gaelic language and culture as barbarous. So he was already prejudiced against the MacDonalds as Gaelic speakers as well as suspected Catholics, and was apparently bribed with promises of the income to be obtained from the lands of Kintyre and Islay. He therefore agreed to the appointment of Sir John Campbell of Cawdor to 'pacify' Islay. The elderly MacDonald chief, Angus, wrote at least twice to James offering in the humblest terms to obey his commands and pay all taxes due, but in 1612 he was obliged to sign away his rights in Islay to John Campbell for what Fraser-Mackintosh calls the 'trifling sum' of 6,000 marks. Soon afterwards, Angus died and was succeeded by his son, Sir James MacDonald, who escaped from prison in Edinburgh Castle, where he had been held since 1604, and raised his standard on Islay. His brother Angus briefly recaptured Dunyvaig

Castle from the Campbells, but the rebellion gained little support and James fled to Spain. Fraser-Mackintosh records with some satisfaction that although the Campbells remained in control of Islay, they never made a penny in profit from it. This was the end of Clan Donald South as a political power, but one of their descendants, Alasdair Mac Colla Chiotaich, later took a bloody revenge. He and his Irish Brigade fought alongside the marquis of Montrose in his civil war campaign of 1644–5, and Alasdair gained a reputation as a skilful and innovative general. He boasted that he never left a Campbell house unburned, and at the Battle of Inverlochy, his troops played a decisive role in the defeat of a Covenanter army under Sir Duncan Campbell of Auchinbreck. The Campbell levies were massacred and Sir Duncan was executed after the battle, allegedly by Alasdair himself.

The MacIains never fully recovered from their defeat at Creag an Airgid, but they held on in Ardnamurchan and a contingent fought with the Clanranalds at Blar na Leine. Around the end of the century, a marriage arrangement gave the nominal feudal overlordship of Ardnamurchan to Archibald Campbell of Argyll, and although for a while the MacIains continued to live as an independent clan, they soon became victims of a similar confidence trick to that played on their cousins of Dunyvaig. In 1602, their chief was induced to acknowledge himself as Argyll's vassal in return for promises of protection. The details of subsequent proceedings are unclear, but as Donald Gregory says, there is more than a suspicion that the Campbells had not acted in good faith. By 1615, Mingary Castle was in the hands of a certain Donald Campbell, who was treating the MacIains as his tenants, and by Gregory's account, treating them very harshly. Fraser-Mackintosh also quotes several testimonials to his 'cruelty and rapacity'. Not surprisingly, the MacIains took to arms, and in 1618, they expelled the Campbells with the help of the Clanranalds. These events were taking place against the background of the great revolt of the MacDonalds of Islay, so the government in Edinburgh was not well disposed towards any of the branches of the clan, and ordered Donald Campbell to be reinstated. In 1624, when the MacIains continued to resist, a warrant was issued for the arrest of their leaders. According to Gregory, 'five or six score' of the clansmen then seized an English ship and took to piracy, eventually collecting a small fleet and becoming for a time 'the terror of the whole west coast of Scotland from Islay northward'. Eventually, government ships caught up with them off Skye and they were forced to abandon their vessels and take refuge in the woods on the Moidart coast, where they were dispersed with the assistance of their old enemies the MacLeods. The survivors seem to have joined the Clanranalds or the Camerons, and after that, Clan MacIain disappears from the records. From then on, Ardnamurchan, like Islay, became Campbell territory.

The Clanranalds, Glengarrys and Keppochs fared better in the short term, and during the seventeenth century, Clan Ranald was fairly prosperous, but the persistent support of all these branches for the Jacobite cause led to their ruin after the defeat of the rising of 1745. The last enduring legacy of the chiefs of Clan Ranald, according to the Statistical Account of Scotland, was to introduce the potato into the Highlands, sometime around 1743. By the 1620s, the MacDonalds of Sleat had eclipsed their southern cousins and become the most powerful branch of the clan. For most of this time they were at daggers drawn with the Clanranalds. They lost their estates temporarily for their support of the Jacobites, but managed to regain royal favour and stayed aloof in 1745.

The Mackays were largely converted to Presbyterianism during the sixteenth century. They continued to resist the encroachments of the Sutherlands, but in the 1580s, civil dissension broke out among them and the Aberach branch defected to the Sutherland camp. In 1589, a marriage was arranged between Huistean Dubh, thirteenth chief of the Strath Naver Mackays, and the daughter of Earl Gordon of Sutherland, and with the partial resolution of the feud between the two houses the Mackay fighting men began to look for alternative employment. In the same year, a combined force of Sutherlands, Mackays and MacLeods from Assynt attacked the Sinclair earl of Caithness, who had been at feud with the Sutherlands. In what became known as '*La na Creach Mor*', 'the Day of the Great Raid', the allied clans sacked the town of Wick and forced the earl to take refuge in his castle at Girnigoe. But this was among the last of the major disturbances in the far north. Early in the following century, Huistean's son Sir Donald Mackay of Farr raised a regiment from his clansmen, which fought with distinction on the Protestant side in the Thirty Years War in Europe, and in 1628, he received from the Scottish Crown the title of Lord Reay. Since then the ancestral territory of the Mackays has often been known as the Reay Country. However, when King Gustavus Adolphus of Sweden was killed in 1632, Lord Reay lost any chance of obtaining a large sum of money that was due to him, and was forced to sell Strath Naver to the Sutherlands to pay his debts. It was often said that the Mackays were far more expert at war than they were at finance or diplomacy (Macdougall, 1953), and this was just the start of a long process by which the neighbours of the impoverished clan gained by purchase the lands they had never been able to take by the sword. Despite their longstanding loyalty to the Stuart monarchy, the Mackays supported the Glorious Revolution that expelled the Catholic James VII (James II of England), and in 1689 General Hugh Mackay commanded the government forces that were defeated by the Jacobites at the battle of Killiecrankie. The clan continued to support the government in the 1715 and 1745 risings, and in March 1746 an incident occurred at Tongue, which provides an interesting footnote to our story (see the detailed account in Duffy, 2015).

A French ship in Jacobite service, *Le Prince Charles* (actually a captured Royal Navy sloop, formerly HMS *Hazard*, with fourteen guns), ran aground at the mouth of the Kyle of Tongue while trying to escape from its pursuers, and in a brief artillery duel with the twenty-gun HMS *Sheerness*, which was watched by the then Lord Reay from his house in Tongue village, the Jacobite crew suffered heavy casualties. The survivors then abandoned ship. But on board *Le Prince Charles* was a cargo that its captain was reluctant to abandon – a consignment of arms for the Jacobite army, plus £13,000 in gold coins (over £1.5 million at today's values), intended for Prince Charles Stuart to pay his men. The crew got the gold ashore in five chests under cover of darkness, and set out with the idea of smuggling it to Caithness, where Jacobite sympathisers were in control. By sheer luck, they found a local man favourable to their cause, who provided them with a guide and horses to carry the chests. They then proceeded down the western side of the Kyle of Tongue towards Ben Loyal before turning eastwards at the mouth of the inlet. Meanwhile, Lord Reay had sent messengers to muster the local militia companies, which intercepted the *Prince Charles*'s crew near the shores of Loch Hakon, more or less on the site of the great Mackay triumph at the Battle of Druim na Coub (Chapter 4). Here there was a brief skirmish and most of the Jacobites were captured, but not before they had opened the treasure chests and scattered the coins in all directions in a desperate attempt to deny them to the enemy. In the ensuing stampede, Lord Reay eventually retrieved slightly more than half of the gold, which he distributed as spoils of war to the officers and men involved as well as to his own family. The rest was never found. Duffy quotes contemporary documents to the effect that 'the happiest man' among the Mackays was one who got away with an intact chest, but many others also seem to have done very well out of the affair. Until this day, people have searched the area and even tried diving in Loch Hakon in the hope of finding more coins, but it is not likely that many still remain. For the Jacobites the business was of course a disaster, which in the view of Angus Mackay (1906) contributed significantly to their defeat at Culloden in the following month.

Like the Campbells, the Mackenzies continued to align themselves with the monarchy, while ensuring that they profited as much as possible from their loyalty. In the aftermath of their victory at Blar na Parc they were granted large parts of the dissolved earldom of Ross, which increased their power without antagonising their immediate neighbours, and their chiefs were always careful to obtain royal charters confirming their possessions. This policy paid off in 1544, when the earl of Huntly tried to recruit the Mackenzies against the Clanranalds. The Mackenzie chief refused to join the war, so Huntly ordered the Grants, Macintoshes and Rosses to attack them. This they unanimously refused to do, and it seems that no subsequent royal lieutenant ever tried to issue orders to the Mackenzies, leaving them, in effect, answerable only to the Crown (Dunlop, 1953). But what really secured the clan's position in the north was the affair of the Fife Adventurers. In the 1590s, internal feuds among the MacLeods of Lewis reduced the island to such chaos that James VI decided to intervene. His response was typical of the attitude of the Lowland Scots of the day towards the Highlanders. He established a consortium of wealthy men, who came to be called the Fife Adventurers from the place of origin of many of them, and granted them possession of Lewis. The procedure has been likened then and since to the colonisation of Native American lands across the Atlantic in its absolute disregard of the rights of the existing inhabitants. But the MacLeods fought back so successfully that by 1607, the Adventurers had given up and gone home. So the king called on Kenneth Mackenzie of Kintail, who it seems had been secretly assisting the MacLeods with just this end in view (Dunlop), to pacify the island once and for all. This he did, defeating the MacLeods and bringing Lewis under his control, for which service he was raised to the peerage with the title of Lord Mackenzie of Kintail. In 1623, his son Colin became the first earl of Seaforth. The seventeenth century saw the Mackenzies continue to enjoy royal favour and become the most powerful of all the clans north of Argyll, but unlike the Campbells, they remained loyal to the Stuart dynasty, and following the defeat of the 1745 uprising, most of their estates were forfeited.

After the final defeat of the Jacobite cause at the Battle of Culloden in 1746, the military history of the clans was over. In reality, they had not existed as independent political entities for some time, but all, Jacobites and government loyalists alike, were now caught up in momentous economic changes as well. With the suppression of the old stock rustling habits of the Highlanders, and the introduction of new breeds from England, sheep farming became big business. (It is probably not coincidence that this happened shortly after the final disappearance of the wolf from Scotland, which is traditionally dated to 1743 but probably occurred a few decades earlier.) As the chiefs no longer needed, or were permitted, to maintain armed followings, they found it more productive to turn over the land to sheep grazing, and the ancient concept of mutual support between the chiefs and their clan relatives was so far eroded that most of them saw their people merely as unprofitable tenants and evicted them en masse. Several of the chiefs, such as Sir Alexander MacDonald of Sleat, went so far as to kidnap their own clansmen and others and sell them into indentured servitude – virtual slavery – in the Americas. Some of the descendants of the warriors of old clung on in the Highlands, while others scraped a living in newly founded fishing ports along the coast like Tobermory. The most notorious example of the Clearances occurred in the early nineteenth century, when the Duke and Countess of Sutherland evicted the Mackays from Strath Naver in an ignominious conclusion to their centuries of rivalry.

In the mid nineteenth century, the potato blight arrived in the Highlands, and while the death and depopulation were not quite as bad as in Ireland, they added greatly to the impoverishment of the people. The Highland regiments of the British Army continued to provide an outlet for their warrior traditions, and a glance at the records of these regiments in the wars of Empire and two world wars will show that the fighting prowess of the Highlanders was by no means diminished. But most of their kin were obliged to emigrate to the Lowland cities or to America, leaving the countryside largely empty. One result of these upheavals, combined with modern education and communications, is that in the course of the last century the Gaelic language has almost died out. The Scottish government and many individual enthusiasts are making heroic efforts to preserve and revive it, but there are few places today, even in the Hebrides, where first language speakers are not in a small minority. The loss of Gaelic accentuates the sense that the heyday of the clans now belongs to a vanished world, and it is hard to imagine today that the tranquil glens were ever the scene of bloody conflicts, or that the ancestors of the hospitable people who still live there were once a source of terror to their neighbours. But the landscape itself is relatively little changed, and in many places it is still possible to gain a vivid impression of what they were like when the banners of the Lord of the Isles flew in sleek black galleys, and mail-clad warriors trod the heather. A few of these places are featured in this book, but the history of the Highlands and Islands is complex and still relatively little studied, especially as far as battlefield archeology is concerned. There are certainly many discoveries still to be made.

Sources and Further Reading

Some of the sources quoted in this book are chronicles written within a century or so of the events they describe. Others are local or clan histories published between the eighteenth and early twentieth centuries, at a time when oral tradition may still have preserved knowledge that is now lost. None of these, however, can be considered as true primary sources. We have no eyewitness accounts of any of the battles featured, even though the narratives relate numerous incidents that, if true, can only have been derived originally from such accounts. Therefore I have not followed the usual convention of dividing the bibliography into 'primary' and 'secondary' works, despite the fact that not all are of equal value, and that many more recent accounts are obviously derived (as of course is this one) from older ones which those making use of them had no means of checking.

Anonymous, *The History of the Feuds and Conflicts Among the clans in the Northern Parts of Scotland and in the Western Isles: From the Year MXXXI unto MDCXIX*, Glasgow, 1780 (cited as 'Conflicts of the Clans').

Archibald, M., *Dance If Ye Can: A Dictionary of Scottish Battles*, Creativia, Helsinki, 2016.

Barrow, G., *Scotland and its Neighbours in the Middle Ages*, London, 1992.

Bingham, C., *Beyond the Highland Line: Highland History and Culture*, London, 1991.

Broun, D. & MacGregor, M. (eds.), *Miorun Mor nan Gall, 'The Great Ill-Will of the Lowlander'?*, Glasgow, 2007

Boswell, James, *The Journal of a Tour to the Hebrides with Samuel Johnson*, London, 1786.

Caldwell, D., 'Having the Right Kit: West Highlanders Fighting in Ireland', in Duffy (ed.), *The World of the Galloglass*, Four Courts Press, 2007.

Campbell, D., *A Treatise on the Language, Poetry and Music of the Highland Clans*, Edinburgh, 1862.

Cannan F., *Scottish Arms and Armour*, Shire Publications, Oxford, 2009.

Cannan, F. & O'Brogain, S., *Galloglass 1250–1600*, Osprey Warrior 143, Oxford, 2010.

Carlton, C., *This Seat of Mars: War and the British Isles, 1485–1746*, Yale University Press, 2011.

Clark, W., *The Lord of the Isles Voyage*, Leinster Press, Naas, Co. Kildare, 1993.

Cooper, J. & Turner, G., *Scottish Renaissance Armies 1513–1550*, Osprey Elite 167, Oxford, 2008.

Cowan, R., 'More Like Lions Than Men: The Battle of Loch Lochy, 1544', *Medieval Warfare* 6.3, 2017, accessed via Wikipedia article, 'Battle of the Shirts'.

Crawford, B., *The Northern Kingdoms: Orkney and Caithness from AD 870 to 1470*, Edinburgh, 2013.

Darling, F. & Boyd, J., *The Highlands and Islands*, Glasgow, 1964.

Dixon, J., *Gairloch in North-West Ross-shire*, Edinburgh, 1886.

Dodgson, R., *From Chiefs to Landlords: Social and Economic Change in the Western Highlands and Islands*, Edinburgh, 1998.

Donaldson, M.E.M., *Further Wanderings, Mainly in Argyll*, Paisley, 1926.

Drummond, J., *Memoirs of Sir Ewen Cameron of Locheill*, MacKnight, J. (ed.), Edinburgh, 1842.

Duffy, C., *Fight for a Throne: The Jacobite '45 Reconsidered*, Helion & Co., Solihull, 2015.

Dunlop, J., *The Clan Mackenzie, Johnston & Bacon Clan Histories*, Edinburgh, 1953.

Durham, K., *Border Reiver 1513–1603*, Osprey Warrior 154, Oxford, 2011.

Dwelly, E., *The Illustrated Gaelic-English Dictionary* (8th ed.), Glasgow, 1973.

Eyre-Todd, G., *The Highland Clans of Scotland: their History and Traditions*, New York, 1923.

Fraser, C., *The Clan Fraser of Lovat, Johnston & Bacon Clan Histories*, Edinburgh, 1952.

Fraser, C., *The Clan Cameron, Johnston & Bacon Clan Histories*, Edinburgh, 1953.

Fraser, James, *Polichronicon Seu Policratica Temporum, or The True Genealogy of the Frasers, c.1666*. Reprinted as *Chronicles of the Frasers*, W. Mackay (ed.), Edinburgh, 1905.

Fraser, William, *The Sutherland Book*, Edinburgh, 1892.

Fraser-Mackintosh, C., *The Last MacDonalds of Isla*, Glasgow, 1895.

Goodwin, G., *Fatal Rivalry: Flodden 1513*, London, 2013.

Gordon, Sir Robert, *A Genealogical History of the Earldom of Sutherland, 1639*. Reprinted by George Ramsay & Co, Edinburgh, 1813.

Grannd, S., *Gaidhlig Dhuthaich Mhic Aoidh, The Gaelic of the Mackay Country*, Melness, Sutherland, 2013.

Grant, A., 'The Wolf of Badenoch', in Sellar, W. (ed.), *Moray, Province and People*, Edinburgh, 1993.

Grant, I., *The Clan Donald, Johnston & Bacon Clan Histories*, Edinburgh, 1952.

Grant, I., *The Clan MacLeod, Johnston & Bacon Clan Histories*, Edinburgh, 1953.

Grant, N., *The Medieval Longsword*, Osprey Weapon 48, Oxford, 2020.

Gregory, D., *History of the Western Highlands and Isles of Scotland*, Edinburgh, 1836.

Gunn, A. & Mackay, J., *Sutherland and the Reay Country*, Glasgow, 1897.
Hallam-Baker, C., *The Battle of Flodden: Why and How*, The Remembering Flodden Project, Branxton, Northumberland, 2012.
Hayes-McCoy, G., *Scots Mercenary Forces in Ireland*, Dublin, 1937.
Haylett, J., *The Battle of Creag an Airgid*, 2014, accessed at clanMaclain.com (from Home page, go to Clan MacIain, then History of Ardnamurchan, 2nd page, 'The Battle of Creag an Airgid').
Heath, I., *Armies of the Middle Ages*, Volume 1, Worthing, 1982.
Henderson, A., 'Ardnamurchan Place Names', *The Celtic Review*, Vol. 10, No. 38, Edinburgh, 1915.
Hill, J. & Freiberg, J., *The Medieval Fighting Man: Costume and Equipment 800–1500*, Crowood Press, Marlborough, 2015.
Hunter, J., *Last of the Free: A History of the Highlands and Islands of Scotland*, Edinburgh, 1999.
Johnson, Samuel, *A Journey to the Western Islands of Scotland*, London, 1775.
Kinsley, J., *The Poems of William Dunbar*, Oxford, 1979.
Laing, D. (ed.), 'Facsimile of an Ancient Heraldic Manuscript Emblazoned by Sir David Lyndsay of the Mount, Lyon King of Arms, 1542', Edinburgh, 1878.
Lamb, H., *Climate: Past, Present and Future*, London, 1977.
Leslie, John, Bishop of Ross, *The History of Scotland, From the Death of James I*, Thomson, T. (ed.), Edinburgh, 1830.
Lindesay of Pitscottie, Robert, *The History and Chronicles of Scotland*, Edinburgh, 1814.
Loades, M., *Swords and Swordsmen*, Barnsley, 2010.
Loades, M., *War Bows*, Oxford, 2019.
MacDonald, C., *Moidart, or Among the Clanranalds*, Edinburgh, 1889.
MacDougall, M., *The Clan Mackay*, *Johnston & Bacon Clan Histories*, Edinburgh, 1953.
MacGregor, M., 'Warfare in Gaelic Scotland in the Later Middle Ages', in Spiers et al (eds.), *A Military History of Scotland*, 2012.
Mackay, Angus, *The Book of Mackay*, Edinburgh, 1906.
Mackay, D., *Clan Warfare in the Scottish Highlands*, Paisley, 1922.
Mackay, J., *The Romantic Story of the Highland Garb and the Tartan*, Stirling, 1924.
Mackay, Robert, *History of the House and Clan of Mackay*, Edinburgh, 1829.
Mackenzie, A., *History of the Mackenzies*, Inverness, 1894.
Mackenzie, A., *History of the Munros of Fowlis*, Inverness, 1898.
Mackinnon, D., *The Clan Ross*, *Johnston & Bacon Clan Histories*, Edinburgh, 1957.
MacLean, J., *A History of the Clan MacLean*, Cincinnati, 1889.
MacLeod, R., *The MacLeods of Dunvegan*, Edinburgh, 1927.
MacLeod, W., 'Images of Scottish Warriors in later Irish Bardic Poetry', in Duffy, S. (ed.), *The World of the Galloglass*, Four Courts Press, Dublin, 2007.

Macrae, D., *The Clan Macrae, Johnston & Bacon Clan Histories*, Edinburgh, 1970.
Major, John, *A History of Greater Britain* (1521), trans A. Constable, reprinted Edinburgh 1892.
Martin Martin, *A Description of the Western Isles of Scotland*, London, 1703. Reprinted (Withers, C. & Munro, R., eds.) Edinburgh, 1999.
Matheson, A., *Scotland's North West Frontier*, Matador, Beauchamp, Leicester, 2014.
Melville, N., *The Two-Handed Sword*, Pen & Sword, Barnsley, 2018.
Miller, J., *The Gathering Stream: The Story of the Moray Firth*, Edinburgh, 2012.
Moffat, A., *The Highland Clans*, London, 2010.
Molloy, B. (ed.), *The Cutting Edge: Studies in Ancient and Medieval Combat*, Stroud, Gloucestershire, 2007.
Monro, D., 'A Description of the Occidental', in *Western Islands of Scotland Circa 1695*, Edinburgh. Reprinted in Martin Martin (Withers, C. & Munro, R., eds.), Edinburgh 1999.
Murray, J., *Reading the Gaelic Landscape, Dunbeath*, Caithness, 2019.
Nicholls, K., 'Scottish Mercenary Kindreds in Ireland, 1250–1600', in Duffy, S. (ed.), *The World of the Galloglass*, Four Courts Press, Dublin, 2007.
Peers, C., *The Highland Battles: Warfare on Scotland's Northern Frontier in the Early Middle Ages*, Pen & Sword, Barnsley, 2020.
Rackham, O., *Woodlands*, London, 2015.
Reese, P., *Flodden: A Scottish Tragedy*, Edinburgh, 2003.
Reid, S., *Scottish National Dress and Tartan*, Shire Publications, Oxford, 2013.
Reid, S. & Turner, G., *Castles and Tower Houses of the Scottish Clans 1450–1650*, Osprey Fortress 46, Oxford, 2006.
Ritchie, J., *The Influence of Man on Animal Life in Scotland*, Cambridge, 1920.
Rixson, D., *The West Highland Galley*, Edinburgh, 1998.
Rixson, D., *Knoydart: A History*, Edinburgh, 2011.
Roberts, J., *Lost Kingdoms: Celtic Scotland and the Middle Ages*, Edinburgh, 1997.
Ross, J., Ross, C., & Ross, A., *The Great Clan Ross*, Clan Ross Association of Canada, Montreal, 1968.
Sadler, J., *Clan Donald's Greatest Defeat: The Battle of Harlaw 1411*, Stroud, Gloucestershire, 2005.
Sadler, J., *Blood on the Wave: Scottish Sea Battles*, Edinburgh, 2010.
Sadler, J. & Serdiville, R., *The Battle of Flodden 1513*, Stroud, Gloucestershire, 2012.
Sage, D., *Memorabilia Domestica, Or Parish Life in the North of Scotland*, Edinburgh, 1889.
Scott Thompson, C., Grosse, H., Pfrenger, K. & Gustitis, R., *Scorners of Death: Fighting Skills of the Medieval Gaelic Warrior*, Fallen Rook Publishing, Glasgow, 2018.
Short, W., *Viking Weapons and Combat Techniques*, Yardley, Pennsylvania, 2009.

Simms, K., 'Images of the Galloglass in Poems to the MacSweeneys', in Duffy, S. (ed.), *The World of the Galloglass*, Four Courts Press, Dublin, 2007.
Skene, W.F., *Celtic Scotland*, Edinburgh, 1880.
Smout, C., 'The History and the Myth of Scots Pine', 2014, accessed at www.scottishforestrytrust.org.uk.
Spiers, E., Crang, J. & Strickland, M. (eds.), *A Military History of Scotland*, Edinburgh, 2012.
Stevenson, D., *Alasdair MacColla and the Highland Problem in the Seventeenth Century*, Edinburgh, 1980.
Stretton, M., 'Piercing Plate Armour With Arrows: Empirical Testing at Bosworth Battlefield Centre', 2018.
Strickland, M., & Hardy, R., *The Great Warbow*, Stroud, 2005.
Younger, P., 'Crouching Enemy, Hidden Ally: The Decisive Role of Groundwater Discharge Features in Two Major British Battles, Flodden 1513 and Prestonpans 1745', in Rose, E. & Mather, J. (eds), *Military Aspects of Hydrogeology*, Geological Society, London, 2012.

Index